Rich Nation / Poor Nation

Why Some Nations Prosper While Others Fail

Dr. Robert Genetski

Published by FastPencil Publishing

First Edition

Table of Contents

This book is dedicated to the miracle of the Rosary and to my grandchildren Alex, Jordon, Mikaela, Ellie, Catie, Adelai, Kaelyn, Danny, Ryleigh and Lauren. May the knowledge and work of your generation advance the spiritual and material well-being of all.

❧

Introduction

The most important issue in economics is why some nations are wealthy while others are poor. Providing policymakers and advocates with the answer to this question can help to raise living standards and reduce poverty throughout the world.

Two and half centuries ago, Adam Smith answered the question by explaining how economic freedom was the key force in determining the wealth of nations. In 1980, Milton Friedman illustrated the power of freedom and free markets in his book and TV series *Free to Choose*. Smith and Friedman provided anecdotal evidence showing how people prospered in free countries, but suffered greatly in countries without such freedom.

Anecdotal examples can provide important insights into the wealth and poverty of nations. However, a more systematic, policy-oriented history of the creation and destruction of wealth among countries can provide both greater insights and more persuasive evidence.

In recent years there has been an outpouring of new data and information bearing on this very issue. Economists and statisticians have painstakingly sought to provide better measures of both economic progress and economic freedom throughout the world. Their work has led to important new data and information as well as many academic studies using this new information.

In spite of a massive amount of new data, there has been no popular, systematic analysis of the implications this data for the wealth and poverty of nations. This book provides such an analysis of the implications of this data.

Thomas Piketty's book, *Capital* in the *Twenty-First Century*, is an example of a popular analysis using some of the new data. Unfortunately, Piketty doesn't attempt to address the question of how nations generate wealth. Instead, Piketty focuses on the *distribution* of wealth. His work is devoted to measuring, explaining and criticizing the inequitable distribution of wealth both within and among various countries.

As with many economists, Piketty assumes the creation of wealth simply happens as a result of innovations. His main contribution to explaining the creation of wealth is one sentence— *Knowledge and skill diffusion is the key to overall productivity growth as well as the reduction of inequality both within and between countries.*

Saying *knowledge* and *skill diffusion* are the keys to creating wealth misses the key issue. The creation of wealth is an extremely complex process. Knowledge, skills and innovation are only a few of the many elements associated with this process. In order to begin to understand the impact of economic policies on wealth, we must first fully understand the process itself.

Focusing on the distribution of income and wealth can lead us to miss the forest for the trees. For example, Piketty refers to the sharp reduction in inequality in the US from 1913 to 1948 as good news. As I show in my analysis, this period includes the worst economic performance in US history. The *good news* of a reduction in income inequality was certainly lost on the poor souls standing in line at soup kitchens during the Great Depression.

There are other fundamental problems with focusing on greater equality of incomes as a policy objective. To begin with, wealth must first be created before it can be distributed. Inequality of incomes is a natural consequence of the successful creation of wealth. When a country prospers and incomes rise, the gap between those with more income and wealth and those with no income and wealth becomes progressively larger. This isn't economics. It's math.

One consistent conclusion from my analysis is how destructive Piketty's recommendations of higher taxes would be for any country foolish enough to pursue them.

The approach in this book is first to define the concept of wealth, and then to describe the process by which wealth is created and destroyed. The next step is to establish criteria for policies associated with the concept of economic freedom. These criteria help us to quantify the extent to which specific government policies either advance or retard freedom. Given the appropriate definitions and criteria for policies, we can proceed to observe the extent to which changes in these policies have been associated with either the creation or destruction of wealth.

The analysis of wealth in the United States goes into more detail than for other countries. This is due to the availability of more detailed historical data as well as to my greater familiarity with US policies and data. For countries outside the US there is a broad overview of policies and economic performance. The overview relies mainly on historical measures of economic freedom provided by the Fraser Institute and the Heritage Foundation. Measures of economic conditions rely on estimates of output per person based on data from the International Monetary Fund and Angus Maddison's *The World Economy.*

Throughout this book, the primary focus of the analysis is on long-term growth trends. There is no attempt to deal with short-term cyclical movements in the economy. Short-term changes in business conditions are often associated more with changes in monetary policy than with changes in government spending, regulations and taxes. Monetary policy and its impact on business cycles is a topic for another book.

With respect to terminology, the words nation and country are used interchangeably, as are the terms classical principles and free-market classical principles. The latter terms denote a specific set of policies designed to promote economic freedom described in previous works by the author.

For purposes of readability, sources, data and notes regarding the data are placed in the data appendix and on the author's website — classicalprinciples.com [http://www.classicalprinciples.com/].

CHAPTER 1

Organization and Summary

Perfect freedom is as necessary to the health and vigor of commerce as it is to the health and vigor of citizenship. — Patrick Henry

Why are some nations rich and others poor? Why do some rich nations, such as the US, at certain times enjoy periods of strong growth and prosperity, while at other times struggle with little or no growth?

These are the very questions economists have attempted to answer for at least two and a half centuries. To be useful, any attempts to answer these questions should be policy oriented. They should provide policymakers and advocates with a clear, practical guide to policies that promote the creation of wealth, as well as those that impede it.

One potential policy-oriented answer is the one provided by the world's two most famous economists— Adam Smith and Milton Friedman. Both viewed economic freedom as the key to the wealth of nations. Economic freedom involves placing the main power and authority over economic issues with individuals instead of with government.

An alternative policy for enhancing wealth is to give more power and control over economic decisions to government. Increasing the government's power and authority over economic decisions produces a corresponding decrease in the economic freedom of individuals. This alternative policy direction has been termed progressivism, socialism and communism, depending on the degree to which government controls economic decisions.

The underlying assumption behind increasing government control over economic decisions is the belief that governments make better decisions than individuals operating in a free market environment. With the collapse of the Soviet Union there has been a greater recognition of the problems associated with the extreme lack of economic freedom under communism. There is less widespread recognition of how less extreme moves to restrict freedom, from either progressive or socialist policies, might also erode wealth and promote poverty. Analyzing the economic performance of various countries under different policy regimes can provide insights into this important issue.

The objective of this book is to provide systematic, historical evidence of the extent to which policies promoting or impeding economic freedom have been associated with the rise and fall of the wealth of nations. Chapter 2 defines wealth in a specific way and explains why the definition is important. In order to measure and test economic concepts it's important to clearly define the terms involved.

Chapter 3 describes the wealth-creation process. It's necessary to describe this process since too often there is a belief that wealth is a natural consequence of technological innovations or is something that can be created by increasing government spending. Chapter 4 deals with measuring the concept of wealth, its relationship to wages, and how best to compare the wealth of one nation to others.

Chapter 5 focuses on the extreme differences between the world's wealthiest and poorest nations. It explains why attempts to redistribute wealth cannot be an effective means to reduce poverty. It also discusses the only practical solution to minimize poverty throughout the world. Chapter 6 summarizes the broad overall relationship between economic freedom and wealth among countries.

Chapter 7 begins the process of looking at the evidence for the creation of wealth in specific countries. The objective is to determine the extent to which economic progress, or a lack of progress, is related to a specific set of policies. The United States is the first, and most unique, example of a country founded on the principles of economic freedom.

The next six chapters are devoted to major shifts in economic policies during the past century in the United States. Periods where policies moved clearly in the direction of economic freedom are distinguished from those where policies moved away from these principles and toward the progressive or socialist agenda.

The most significant finding from this analysis is that no growth in wages occurred during those periods when economic polices moved in the direction of the progressive agenda. Almost all gains in workers' wages since 1900 occurred during years when US policies embraced free-market classical principles. This finding explains how the disappointing performance of wages from 2004-2015 is not unusual. It is typical of every historical period when economic policies have enhanced the power and control of government at the expense of individual economic freedom.

The remaining chapters analyze economic performance in countries throughout the world. Chapter 14 compares wealth in the United States to Canada, Australia, and New Zealand. Chapter 15 compares the United States to Europe's wealthiest countries. The three —Norway, Switzerland and Ireland—provide important lessons regarding the European experience with creating wealth.

Chapter 16 describes policies in the two most extreme real world examples of countries following free- market classical principles—Singapore and Hong Kong. Although neither country is blessed with natural resources, each has progressed from being among the poorest nations in the world to being among the world's wealthiest countries.

The next two chapters examine the role of classical principles in the resurgence of growth in China and India. Chapter 19 deals with Russia's failed experiment with communism and its recent attempts to restore growth. Chapter 20 examines how Japan moved from being a world leader in terms of economic growth to a quarter century of economic stagnation.

Chapters 21 and 22 look at recent developments in Latin America and Africa from the perspective of economic freedom. A final chapter summarizes the evidence.

Two and a half centuries after Adam Smith wrote *The Wealth of Nations*, and more than half a century since Milton Friedman updated the case for freedom, our analysis confirms their insights. There is clear, overwhelming evidence over the course of history and throughout the world. The evidence is fully consistent with the conclusion classical economists reached over two centuries ago: Economic freedom is the key to the wealth of nations.

CHAPTER 2

What is Wealth?

I don't want to be a millionaire, I just want to live like one.
— Walter Hagen

Wealth is an elusive concept. While everyone has an idea what it is, it often means different things to different people. When we refer to the wealth of nations, the potential for confusion is even greater.

For purposes of this book, wealth has a specific meaning. Wealth is the value of those goods and services originally created to meet the demands of others. Defined in this way, *wealth* is what determines the living standards of people throughout the world. Since this meaning of wealth differs from the more common meaning, it helps to clarify the difference.

People often view wealth from a personal perspective. Wealthy people—the rich—have substantially more income or assets than we have. The poor have substantially less. One problem with this view is there are various ways to become wealthy that have nothing to do with the creation of wealth. We can inherit wealth. Win it. Steal it. Even marry it. In each of these cases, the wealth was created by someone else.

While hard work and effort can produce wealth, it's not the essential ingredient. Individuals in some of the poorest nations in the world work much harder than those in wealthier nations but have little to show for it. Those who marry into wealth may have worked very hard and sacrificed a great deal. While their efforts can enable them to become personally wealthy, their wealth represents a transfer of something created by others.

A similar distinction can be made for politicians, lawyers and accountants, whose work enables them to become wealthy. These professionals can enhance a nation's wealth when they use their skills to help their clients keep or enhance the wealth they have created. However, politicians, lawyers and accountants can also undermine a nation's wealth when they use their skills to shift wealth from those who created it to others.

The title of P.J. O'Rourke's hilarious book, *Eat the Rich*, captures the resentment some people have for the rich. Most who resent the rich likely do so out of a suspicion their wealth came at someone else's expense. There is seldom resentment for the wealth of famous sports heroes or other celebrities. It's obvious their wealth is the result of their unique talents. They earned it!

It is not always obvious how those running businesses earned their wealth. Without such knowledge, it is easy to assume their financial success came at the expense of others. Resentment of the rich can be justified if wealth was at the expense of others. However, the most successful businesses are those that provide the greatest improvements in the living standards of their customers. Microsoft, Apple, Amazon and Google have made their owners fabulously wealthy by serving the needs of others. They have been among the leading businesses contributing to improving the wealth of their customers and, in turn, the wealth of nations.

Although wealth is usually associated with the accumulation of assets, it isn't a static concept. It's dynamic. Wealth involves an ongoing creative process, one where individuals continually work to provide others with things they value.

All material assets lose most, if not all, of their value when individuals stop producing things. A mansion might one day be worth millions of dollars. Without people constantly working to provide food, water, electricity, security, communications and other essential accompaniments, the mansion's value would quickly plummet. The real value of every asset is tied to the ongoing work of an extensive supporting cast of hardworking people.

Wealthy nations are those whose workers produce significantly more of the things its people value than an average nation. Poor nations are those where workers produce significantly less.

Somewhere around 4,000 B.C. Egypt became the first nation to emerge from the ancient world. Blessed with the Nile's gift of fertile land, Egyptians were the most prosperous people in the world.

Prosperity is a relative concept. In ancient Egypt it meant you had a job (forced labor), sufficient food to sustain yourself and your family, and you were relatively secure from external threats. You and your extended family also lived in the same mud-brick house.

In spite of having a head start on every other nation, Egypt is no longer a rich country. In 2015, the living standard of Egypt's workers was 13% below the world's average.

For over a century the United States had the largest economy in the world in terms of the creation of goods and services. In 2014, China passed the US in terms of overall output and has continued to move ahead. While China's economy is currently the largest in the world, China isn't wealthy. It is, at best, a middle class country.

Of all the world's largest countries, the United States is by far the most productive in terms of providing its people with the greatest amount of goods and services. As a result, its people enjoy the world's highest living standards. However, the United States isn't the most productive nation. In 2015 Singapore's workers produced $85,000 of output per person, well above the $56,000 of the United States. Moreover, while the productivity of certain other countries has recently increased, there are indications productivity in the United States is no longer increasing. From the standpoint of people, changes in a nation's economic condition can be even more important than the level.

There has always been a dynamic ebb and flow of wealth among nations. This ebb and flow provides hope for every nation seeking to enhance the wealth of its citizens. It also provides a warning to successful nations not to take prosperity for granted.

While it takes many generations for a nation to achieve wealth, it can take less than a generation to lose it. Each nation's destiny depends on the ability of its citizens to recognize and embrace the forces that contribute to the original creation of wealth.

The Wealth Creating Process

Golden Rule for prosperity: The best way to become rich is to serve others

There is a fundamental principle behind the creation of wealth—*you receive in proportion to what you give.* This is as true for an individual as it is for a nation.

Workers who acquire above-average skills, and put forth above-average effort, tend to receive above-average earnings. In doing so, they make above-average contributions to their nation's wealth.

People who run successful businesses receive the greatest rewards when their businesses are the most effective at providing the things others want. Those who have the discipline to postpone spending and save for the future build their own wealth, while their savings provide the funds necessary for investments in future growth.

While some people attribute individual wealth accumulation to "luck"; the assertion is generally a convenient excuse for a perceived lack of success on the part of the person making the assertion. Luck may play a role in the accumulation of wealth in a few isolated instances. In the vast majority of success stories, wise choices, dedication, and staying power play a decisive role in the outcome.

Many economists have a naive view of the wealth-creation process. Some claim government spending increases a nation's wealth. Still others believe wealth creation is a natural process that occurs amid periodic outbursts of innovations and technological advancements. As we will see in subsequent chapters, the evidence shows neither view is correct.

While government is essential to providing the proper environment for creating wealth, all wealth is created in the private sector. Every dollar government spends is a dollar that was first earned in the private sector. The spending power associated with those dollars is *transferred* from those who earned it to government.

In most cases the transfer is direct. Government takes the money by taxing the person creating wealth. The transfer from the private sector to government is indirect when government borrows funds from the private sector to support its spending. As with a tax, the funds the government borrows were first earned by those in the private sector. Public spending itself can be indirect; as it is when government orders the private sector to use the funds it earns to comply with certain laws and regulations.

Since all wealth is created in the private sector, it should be apparent governments cannot provide for the original creation of wealth. Government's role is to create the right environment to maximize the wealth-creating forces in the private sector.

For government to make a positive contribution to the creation of wealth, it must spend its funds in a more productive manner than if the funds had been left for use in the private sector. This can happen when government spends to provide for public safety, for a just and efficient legal system as well as other crucial public services. However, without the discipline imposed by a system of profits and losses, there is a strong tendency for government spending to be less efficient than private spending. This is why government-run businesses destroy wealth instead of enhancing it. This is the case whether the example consists of factories run by the old Soviet Union or by China, or Mexico's oil company or the Postal Service in the United States. Government-run businesses tend to deplete a nation's wealth.

The reason for emphasizing the role of the private sector as the original source of all income is not to denigrate the role of government. It is to recognize explicitly the natural constraints on government spending and power. Without the creation of income in the private sector, the public sector cannot exist. Hence, the more government expands its power by reaching deeper into the private sector for its funding, the more government limits the creation of wealth. And the less wealth it can redistribute, the less effective government becomes at achieving its objectives.

The key to the process of creating wealth is to identify the type of system or organization best able to turn innovations into goods and services valued by consumers. Every country in the world has innovators with clever ideas on how to better serve the needs of others. Ideas are the easy part. Turning ideas into reality is the real challenge.

The creation of wealth is an immensely complex process. Many things must come together to fully realize the benefits of innovations and new technologies. Funds are necessary to begin to implement the ideas. Skilled managers need to be brought on to organize the process. Talented, industrious workers have to be hired. There must be a system to provide information about the most efficient uses of various resources for implementing innovations. The system also must be able to assure all necessary resources to complete the project are always in the right place, at the right time and at the right price.

These are daunting tasks, far beyond the talents of any individual or bureaucracy. While new technologies and innovations play a role in increasing wealth, it should be obvious much more is involved. Classical economists explained why a free-market system providing the maximum amount of individual freedom was best able to maximize the wealth-creating process.

For most of recorded history neither individual freedom nor free markets existed. As a consequence, in spite of numerous innovations, living standards were essentially unchanged from the birth of Christ until the latter part of the Middle Ages. It wasn't until around the 14th and 15th centuries that the first glimmers of freedom began to appear in Europe. As individual freedom emerged, so did the first increases in living standards. At first, this relationship appeared tenuous. As subsequent chapters will show, there is substantial evidence to show how individual freedom and free markets are the motivating force—the wellspring—of the wealth of nations.

CHAPTER 4

Measuring the Wealth of Nations

What can be asserted without evidence can also be dismissed without evidence.
— Christopher Hitchens

The first step in understanding why some nations are rich and others poor is to measure wealth. We noted how a nation's wealth results from the ongoing process of creating things other people value. One of the most common measures of this concept is referred to as a nation's gross domestic product or GDP. GDP provides an estimate of the value of all final goods and services produced in a nation during a specific period of time, such as a year. Instead of the pretentious term GDP, from this point on we will refer to GDP simply as a nation's output.

Comparing the wealth of one nation to others involves a number of potential problems. Among these is the issue of converting currencies. Since each country reports its output in its own currency, comparing the wealth or output of one country to that of another involves converting information on output into a common currency.

While currency exchange rates can be used for the adjustment, they don't measure what we want to measure. Exchange rates show how much of one country's currency we can get for the other country's currency at a point in time. This doesn't tell us how living standards or wealth in one country compares to others. For making such comparisons we want to know how many US dollars it would take to purchase a similar basket of goods and services in each country.

For example, if someone in the US can buy a certain basket of goods for $1,000 and someone in another country can buy a similar basket for 500 units of their currency, it means that their currency has twice the purchasing power of a US dollar.

Since the purchasing power of the other country's currency is twice that of the United States, we have to double their output in terms of the other country's currency to make it comparable to US dollars. *Purchasing power parity* (PPP) is the term used to adjust the value of a nation's output from its own currency into US dollars. Happily, such a calculation exists and is widely recognized in economic analysis. In this book, whenever we compare one nation's output, or wealth, to that of another nation we will use the PPP adjustment to make the comparison.

The largest economies in the world are those that produce the most goods and services. The following are world leaders in terms of total economic output.

The World's Largest Economies: 2015

	Output based on PPP (Trillions of dollars)	Percent of the World's Output
China	$19.4	17%
United States	17.9	16
India	8.0	7
Japan	4.8	4
Germany	3.8	3
Russia	3.7	3
Brazil	3.2	3
Indonesia	2.8	2
UK	2.7	2
France	2.6	2

Source: International Monetary Fund, World Economic Outlook Database, April 2016

It's easy to confuse size with wealth. The saying "size matters" doesn't apply when referring to a nation's wealth. China and India are two of the largest economies in the world. Neither is wealthy. These countries produce a lot of output, but each has over a billion people. Dividing a nation's output by its population provides a more meaningful estimate of the wealth of its people.

Output per person, adjusted for PPP, is the most commonly accepted measure for international comparisons of wealth among different countries. It is also a nebulous concept. Few people can relate to it. What most people can relate to are wages or salaries.

For various reasons, it's possible to use output per person as a *rough* approximation of the average annual wage in a country. The data appendix explains why this is so. Hence, whenever you see output per person for any country you can think of it as the average annual wage for the country. Some may prefer to consider the median wage (where there are as many workers earning more as earning less). Reducing the average wage by 20% can provide a rough estimate of the median worker's annual wage.

With this background information we are ready to begin comparing the wealth of various nations.

CHAPTER 5

The World's Richest, Poorest & Middle Class Nations

I've been poor and I've been rich. Rich is better! — Beatrice Kaufman

In 2015, the following nations were the wealthiest in the world. Nations with fewer than roughly five million people and those where oil deposits account for a third or more of their wealth, were not included. With these criteria, Singapore is the wealthiest nation in the world while the United States is the wealthiest of the world's largest countries. Workers in these two countries produce far more goods and services than workers in most other countries. As a result, the people in these countries have the highest living standards in the world.

World's Wealthiest Nations: 2015

	Output per person (PPP)	Population (Millions)
Singapore	$85,253	6
Norway	68,430	5
Switzerland	58,551	8
Hong Kong	56,701	7
United States	55,805	322
Ireland	55,533	5
Netherlands	49,166	17
Sweden	47,922	10
Australia	47,389	24
Austria	47,250	9

Source: International Monetary Fund, World Economic Outlook Database, April 2016

In Norway oil accounts for anywhere from 10% to 25% of total output. Hence, at least some of their wealth is due to these natural resources.

In 2015, the world's population was estimated to be 7.2 billion people. Roughly half of these people lived in countries where output per person was above $14,000. The other half lived in countries with output per person below this level. Hence, the world's middle class countries are those with output per person in the vicinity of this level.

World's Major Middle Class Nations: 2015

	Output per person (PPP)	Population (Millions)
Brazil	$15,615	205
Iraq	15,474	35
Dominican Rep.	14,984	82
Algeria	14,504	40
China	**14,107**	**1375**
Colombia	13,847	48
South Africa	13,165	55
Peru	12,195	32

Source: International Monetary Fund, World Economic Outlook Database, April 2016

In sharp contrast to the extraordinary success of the world's richest nations, and the mediocre performance of others, is the extreme poverty found in those nations where output per person is below these levels. For example, India's 1.3 billion people live in a country where output per person is only half that of Peru. As poor as India is, there are many nations even worse off.

Abject poverty is the inability to earn enough for basic human needs, such as food, water, clothing, and shelter. Many economies perform so poorly they cannot meet the most basic needs of their people. The World Bank estimates there are roughly a billion people who suffer from conditions of abject poverty.

The International Monetary Fund lists the following nations among the poorest of the poor, defined by output per person.

World's Poorest Nations: 2015

	Output per person PPP	Population (millions)
Central African Rep.	$600	5
Dem. Rep. Congo	800	82
Liberia	900	4
Niger	1,100	18
Malawi	1,100	18
Mozambique	1,200	28
Guinea	1,200	12
Eritrea	1,300	7
Madagascar	1,500	24
Togo	1,500	7

Source: International Monetary Fund, World Economic Outlook Database, April 2016

Redistributing Wealth

The extreme difference in wealth between the wealthiest nations, where many live in luxurious surroundings, and the poorest nations, where billions literally starve, is extremely disturbing. Such inequality leads some to conclude those who live in wealthy countries enjoy their benefits at the expense of those who are less fortunate. Many believe social justice requires the redistribution of income from those who have to those in need.

We are called upon by God and our conscience to help those in need. The character of an individual is measured by the extent to which he or she *voluntarily* provides for the needs of others from their own resources. Such voluntary giving can relieve the suffering of certain needy individuals. However, there are simply too many aspects of poverty and too many poor people for redistribution of income to make a significant reduction in the world's poverty.

For example, confiscating 20% of the yearly output from all those in our ten wealthiest countries and redistributing it among those in the bottom half of all nations, it would add only about $1,300 a year to their income. Some of the poor would temporarily have a windfall gain. However, as we will see in subsequent chapters, involuntary redistribution of income permanently reduces *future* output in successful countries. Ultimately, the reduction in wealth in these countries would reduce any future redistribution. Instead of reducing world poverty, involuntary income redistribution increases poverty.

If involuntary redistribution of wealth has any meaning, we must begin by identifying who should give their income to the poor. In other words, who are the rich? From a global standpoint, Mexico produced 35% more output per person in 2015 than the average middle class nation. And yet, Mexico has its own serious problems with poverty.

In the United States, the government classifies an individual as poor if their income is roughly $12,000 a year. A family of four is considered poor if their income is below roughly $24,000 a year. These income levels equate to the middle class or upper middle class in the rest of the world. To combat its *relative* poverty, the United States has more than eighty separate federal programs and spends a trillion dollars a year to help the poor.

While there are always issues about how efficient and effective government programs might be, taxpayers in the US (mainly upper income earners) already have a substantial amount of their income *involuntarily* taken from them for the purpose of helping those in need.

Resources and Need

Estimates from the World Bank show 13% of the world's population, roughly a billion people, live on less than $2 a day. Even more discouraging are estimates showing half the world's population, about 3.6 billion people are classified as truly poor. The problems even rich countries face attempting to help the poor in their own countries shows how redistribution, whether voluntary or involuntary, is simply incapable of making significant progress in reducing the world's poverty.

Fortunately, there is a solution. Poverty can be significantly reduced by giving the poor the same opportunities as those in successful economies. The only practical solution to enhancing the wealth of nations is for poor countries to replicate the formula for success followed by wealthy nations.

The World Bank's estimates of global poverty indicate this has been happening. In 1981, 44% of the world's population lived under conditions of abject poverty, literally starving to death. The percentage fell to 37% in 1990 and was down to 13% in 2012.

These changes were due primarily to policy changes in two large countries—China and India. Those policy changes enabled a billion and a half people to move out of conditions characterized as extreme poverty. Chapters 17 and 18 discuss these policy changes.

The only real hope for significantly reducing worldwide poverty is the widespread application of wealth-enhancing policies. This is why we have a moral obligation to examine the evidence concerning the effectiveness of such policies on the wealth of nations. The next chapter marks the beginning of such an examination.

CHAPTER 6

Economic Freedom and the Wealth of Nations

A society that puts equality before freedom will get neither. A society that puts freedom before equality will get a high degree of both.
— Milton Friedman

People have an innate desire to be free—free to choose how to live their lives, care for their families, pursue their dreams and make the most of their God-given talents. In spite of this innate desire for freedom, through most of recorded history freedom did not exist.

Just as most people have an innate desire to be free, there are those who have an innate desire to control others. When given the opportunity, those who are able to control the actions and decisions of others will generally do so.

From the beginning of recorded history until the Middle Ages, most ordinary people lacked economic and social freedom. They lived according to the dictates of others. Freedom was an alien concept. Decisions of the tribal leader, Pharaoh, King, feudal lord, or religious fanatics controlled the lives and behavior of ordinary people. In spite of numerous innovations designed to increasing living standards, most people lived lives similar to what they were in ancient Egypt.

The first improvement in living standards began in Western Europe during the 14th and 15th centuries. This was also the time in England when parliament began to take power from the throne and establish the rule of law. The rule of law is an essential component for economic freedom. Democracy, perhaps surprisingly, is not. While democracy has many positive traits, fostering economic freedom is not one of them.

In a democracy a majority can vote to limit the freedom of the minority. The majority can pass laws to confiscate the income of a select group and transfer public funds to favored groups, projects or causes. The majority can also vote to control prices, wages or interest rates and impose licensing requirements on people, preventing them from being able to work. In each of these ways, democracies can place limits on individual economic freedom just as effectively as any dictator.

As freedom emerged in Europe, living standards began to improve. The discovery of America proved pivotal in the quest for freedom. Even before gaining its independence from England, the colonies were settled by individuals seeking to gain more control and independence over their lives than they were able to obtain in Europe.

America's independence produced a quantum leap forward in terms of economic freedom. The Founding Fathers were aware of the tendency for those in power to subjugate and control others, so they sought to create a framework to allow freedom to flourish. They did so by containing the power, size and scope of government, and by separating power among the different branches of government.

The US Constitution represented a unique experiment, one which exceeded the hopes and dreams of those who created it. Individual freedom proved to be a powerful magnet. It attracted people from every corner of the world for a taste of this recently discovered elixir. Propelled by a foundation built on individual freedom, the United States began the 20th century as the most powerful economy in the world.

By the beginning of the 21st century, economic freedom had spread to other nations. Two organizations, the Fraser Institute and the Heritage Foundation, attempt to measure the amount of economic freedom in almost every nation in the world. Both organizations measure freedom from the perspective of free-market, classical principles.

Here is the concept of freedom from Fraser's 2015 annual report:

The cornerstones of economic freedom are (1) personal choice, (2) voluntary exchange coordinated by markets, (3) freedom to enter and compete in markets, and (4) protection of persons and their property from aggression by others. Economic freedom is pre-

sent when individuals are permitted to choose for themselves and engage in voluntary transactions as long as they do not harm the person or property of others.

In its 2016 report, Fraser presented economic freedom measures for 159 countries. It then determined the output per person for each quartile. The pattern confirms the conclusions of academic research— nations providing their citizens with greater economic freedom are also those where individuals tend to have higher living standards.

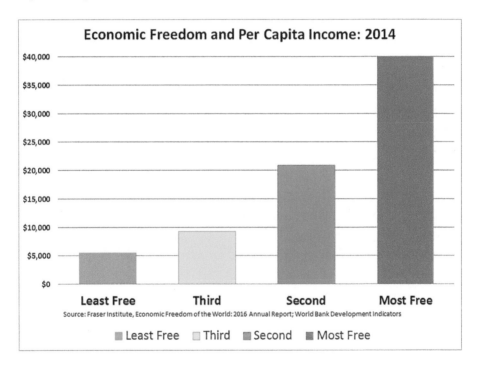

Economic Freedom and Per Capita Income: 2014

Source: Fraser Institute, Economic Freedom of the World: 2016 Annual Report; World Bank Development Indicators

With respect to the poor, there is an even more dramatic difference. Greater degrees of economic freedom tend to produce progressively higher incomes for the poor. This confirms the conclusion Adam Smith reached over two centuries ago, when he wrote how the poor would be those who benefited the most from policies increasing economic freedom.

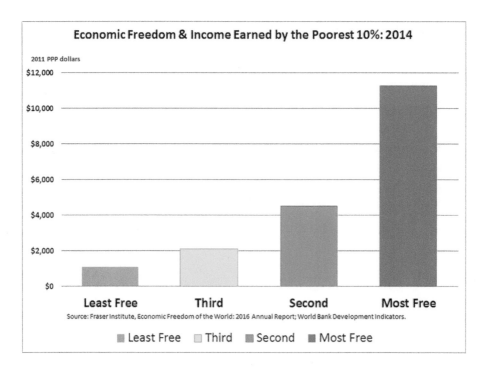

The Fraser data also offer an interesting insight into the relationship between inequality of income and economic freedom. It appears the *share* of income to the lowest 10% of income earners is not directly related to economic freedom. Rather, there is a tendency for the poor to have roughly 2.5% of a country's income irrespective of the degree of economic freedom.

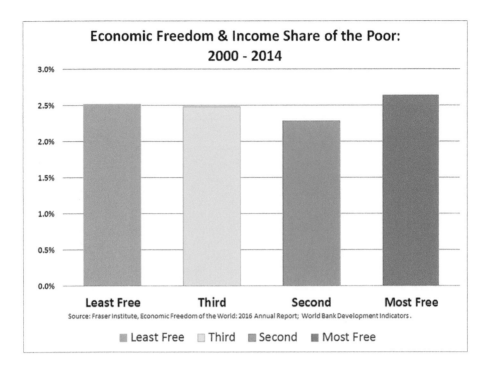

The evidence presented by the Fraser Institute's study strongly suggests economic freedom is a critical factor determining people's living standards. Not only do policies promoting economic freedom boost the living standards of middle-class workers, they also benefit the poor. And they do so without increasing the inequality of income.

Such broad conclusions can be helpful. However, for a better understanding of the relationship between freedom and prosperity, it's necessary to delve more deeply into the specific experiences of individual countries. We should want to know what specific aspects of economic freedom are most important for promoting a nation's wealth, and what happens when policies limit such aspects.

It is also important to assess apparent exceptions to general tendencies. For example, we should look closely at situations where a country's economic freedom score is relatively high, but its output per person is not high. Such exceptions to the general tendency can provide important insights to the source of a nation's wealth.

The following chapters begin this analysis by looking closely at the experience of the country with the longest and most successful history of creating wealth for the greatest number of its people—the United States of America.

CHAPTER 7

The Extraordinary US Economy

Liberty, when it begins to take root, is a plant of rapid growth.
– George Washington

Of all the economies in the world, the United States has the longest, most successful record of improving people's living standards. The foundation for its success lies in its legacy of individual freedom and two and a half centuries of efforts to preserve the institutions that are the source of such freedom.

In declaring its independence from England, the Founding Fathers made it clear they were creating an independent nation subject only to God. They appealed *"to the Supreme Judge of the World"* and sought *"the protection of divine Providence"* for their undertaking. By explicitly referring to the *Creator* as the ultimate source of freedom, they dramatically extended the idea of freedom. Individual freedom was not something granted or denied by government. It was an inalienable, God-given right. Hence, any government failing to recognize this right was illegitimate.

The Founders also understood how government could be the single greatest threat to freedom. To protect against this threat, they included specific restrictions to the government's power and dispersed the power among different branches of government.

The allure of individual freedom attracted people from all over the world. By 1820, living standards in the United States were well above those in the rest of the world, but still behind those in the United Kingdom. By the beginning of the 20th century, the Founder's unique experiment to maximize individual freedom was so successful the United States surpassed the United Kingdom to become the wealthiest nation in the world.

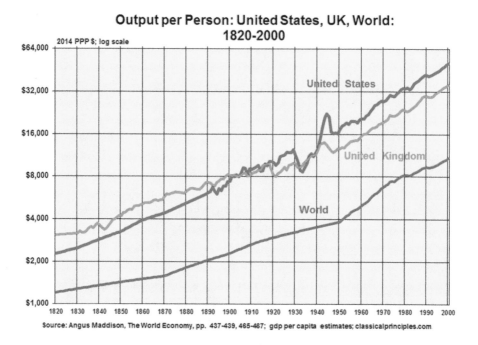

Output per Person: United States, UK, World: 1820-2000

Source: Angus Maddison, The World Economy, pp. 437-439, 465-467; gdp per capita estimates; classicalprinciples.com

From 1900 to 2015, the nation's wealth increased, at an average rate of just over 3% a year. Increases in productivity accounted for slightly more than half of this gain while population growth accounted for the rest. Gains in productivity were sufficient to raise the average yearly wage from $11,600 in 1900 to $59,000 in 2015, a 400% increase.

At first, the limits the Constitution placed on the federal government worked. In 1913, federal spending was less than 2% of the nation's output. However, a century later, federal spending was more than 22%. Federally mandated expenditures brought the total cost of the federal government to more than a third of the nation's output. When state and local government spending and the cost of their mandates are included, the total cost of government amounted to roughly half of the economy's output by 2015.

The combination of a massive expansion of government and strong increases in living standards might suggest the expansion in government was responsible for the increase in wages. It was not. The following chapters will show how neither the expansion of government nor the increase in wages occurred at a steady pace. Rather, there were ongoing cycles as the nation struggled to determine the appropriate size and influence of government.

To assess the economic consequences associated with this struggle it's necessary first to specify two distinct sets of policies. Only then can we assess the impact of these policies on wages and the economy. The term classical defines periods when policies clearly moved in the direction of free-market classical principles; the term progressive defines periods when policies clearly moved away from these principles. The term progressive was originally used during the nation's first move away from free-market classical principles.

Clear descriptions of each term are necessary to identify the specific policies associated with each period.

Characteristics of Classical Economic Periods

Classical economic periods are those where policies move in the direction of enhancing economic freedom. They are periods where the government's control over individuals, businesses and markets is modest or receding.

Specifically, classical periods are those where: 1) federal spending, particularly for nondefense purposes, is either modest or increasing at a slower rate than spending in the rest of the economy; 2) tax rates are either low or are being reduced, particularly for investors, businesses and those with higher incomes; 3) markets are either free to adjust to the pressures or supply and demand or barriers to such adjustments are being reduced; and 4) rules and regulations covering individuals, businesses and markets are minimal or declining.

There is a crucial fifth characteristic of economic freedom—the rule of law must protect individuals and their property. This characteristic can be even more important than the others. Fortunately, the rule of law and protection of property rights has not traditionally been as serious a problem for the United States as in other countries. Unfortunately, the Fraser Institute indicates this tradition may be ending. The Institute's 2015 report on Economic Freedom of the World (EFW) states, *"While the US ratings and rankings have fallen in all five areas of the EFW index, the reductions have been largest in the Legal System and Protection of Property Rights."*

Characteristics of Progressive Economic Periods

Progressive economic periods have characteristics opposite those of classical periods. These are periods where the government's power and control over individuals, businesses and markets are increasing.

Specifically, progressive periods are those where: 1) federal spending, particularly for nondefense purposes, is increasing faster than spending in the rest of the economy; 2) tax rates are either high or increasing, particularly for investors, businesses and those with higher incomes; 3) government prevents markets from freely adjusting to the pressures of supply and demand or barriers to such adjustments are increasing; and 4) rules and regulations for individuals, businesses and markets are either substantial or increasing.

The economic history of the United States from 1913 to 2015 consists of an ongoing conflict over the type of economic policies the nation should adopt. As the following chapters reveal, the choice of policies has had important implications for the nation's economic performance.

The analysis presented in these chapters shows how almost all increases in workers' take-home pay occurred when US policies were moving clearly in the direction of free-market classical principles. In contrast, there were no gains in average take-home pay for the periods when economic policies followed the progressive agenda.

Whenever US policies abandoned classical principles, they mirrored the policies of most other nations in the world. It is insightful to find how during the periods when the US adopted the progressive agenda, the US economy behaved in much the same way as a third-world economy.

The next chapter begins an examination of the details surrounding both policies and their economic impact during the nation's first experiment with progressive economic policies.

CHAPTER 8

Early 20th Century and the Progressive Agenda

No doubt a great deal of nonsense has been talked about the inalienable rights of the individual.... – President Woodrow Wilson

No one provided a more articulate case against an individual's right to freedom than President Woodrow Wilson. He was the undisputed leader of the nation's first progressive movement. Whereas the Founders feared the power of government with its potential to curtail individual freedom, Wilson embraced such power. He was an outspoken critic of both the nation's Founders and the Constitution, writing extensively on the superiority of government over individuals.

Wilson claimed the idea individuals had inalienable rights was nonsense. As with other progressives, he believed expanding the government's size and power would be instrumental to improving people's lives. Wilson saw the Constitution as an impediment to expanding government. He believed the Constitution should be a flexible, living document, capable of changing so as not to constrain policymakers' power over individuals.

The groundwork for enabling the progressive movement came from Republican President William Taft. Upon taking office in March of 1909, Taft's first move was to call on Congress to amend the Constitution to allow government to tax income. Taft also urged the creation of what would become the Federal Reserve to permit government to expand the money supply.

By 1913, ratification of the 16th Amendment gave the federal government the authority to tax income, while passage of the Federal Reserve Act gave it the power to expand and contract the money supply.

These policies dramatically changed the course of US history. Prior to these moves, individuals had almost unfettered power over their economic and financial lives. Their financial livelihood depended primarily on their own skills, efforts and ingenuity. After 1913, their financial livelihood would also depend on how skillfully government policymakers used their vast new powers.

The hubris of progressives such as Wilson stood in stark contrast to the humility of the nation's Founders. Where the Founders called on God for assistance and guidance, progressives were openly hostile to religion. They viewed themselves as superior beings, whose enlightened policies would be capable of creating a heaven on earth.

Upon taking office in March, 1913 Wilson wasted no time in asking Congress to approve a tax on both individual and corporate income. By current standards, tax rates in 1913 were modest, ranging from 1% to 7% of income. They were designed only for millionaires and billionaires as the lowest rate applied to incomes over $500,000 in today's dollars. It wasn't long before a series of tax increases from 1916 through 1918 raised income tax rates from 6% to 77% of income, while lowering the taxable threshold to the equivalent of $37,000 in today's dollars.

As we might expect, the role of the federal government expanded significantly during Wilson's term. From his first budget in 1914 to his last in 1921, non-defense federal spending increased five times faster than spending in the total economy. In addition to higher tax rates and increased government spending, Wilson imposed numerous regulatory burdens on business. He also used government policy in an attempt to control wages and prices, both during and after World War I.

The chart at the end of this chapter shows key economic trends for wages and consumer spending before, during, and after the first period of progressive policies. The upward surge in 1917-18 represents economic activity associated with World War I. Once the war ended, so did the war-time boom. By 1920 most measures of economic activity indicated the strong economic gains the US had experienced prior to 1913 had come to an end. Unfortunately, the economic damage wasn't over.

Four years of the Federal Reserve's highly expansive wartime monetary policy had increased prices by 80%. The Fed reversed a highly expansive monetary policy with a series of large increases in interest rates beginning in October, 1919. The shift to monetary restraint produced a steep recession that lasted from January of 1920 until July of 1921.

The recession contributed to a landslide victory for Republicans in the 1920 elections. The stage was set for a major policy change.

President Warren Harding and then President Calvin Coolidge implemented a classical agenda consisting of significant cuts in tax rates, federal spending and regulations. The Revenue Act of 1921 (most of which took effect in 1922) lowered the top tax rate from 73% to 58% and raised the thresholds for applying each rate. A capital gains tax rate was established. It brought the effective tax rate on capital gains from as high as 73% down to 12.5%. The tax on corporations, which had been as high as 73%, was cut to 10% in 1921 and 12.5% thereafter.

The impact of these tax changes along with a recovery from the recession of 1921 led to an explosive recovery in real growth. Inspired by the gains, policymakers cut taxes again in 1924. The lowest individual tax rate moved from 4% to 2% and the top rate moved from 58% to 46%. The thresholds for applying the rates were also increased by roughly 30%. Still another tax cut in 1926 reduced the lowest rate to 1.5% and the top rate to 25% for incomes over $100,000 in today's dollars. This further reduced effective taxes, particularly for middle and upper income taxpayers.

Government spending was also contained. From 1920 to 1929, while spending in the overall economy increased by 15%, federal spending was cut in half. Taken from its peak in 1918 to its low in 1928, nondefense federal spending was also cut in half.

The reduction in government spending, tax cuts and deregulation of business and markets were accompanied by further gains in the economy. By the end of the decade, this period became known as the *Roaring Twenties.*

In spite of major reductions in the power and influence of the federal government, policymakers were unwilling to reduce the role of the government to where it had been before the Wilson years. Hence, elements of the progressive agenda remained.

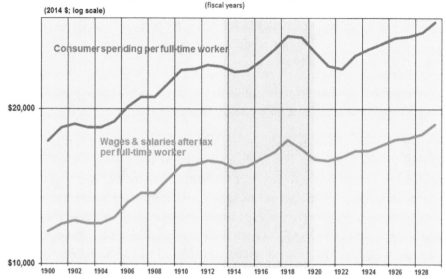

Wages & Consumer Spending: 1900-1929

(2014 $; log scale)   (fiscal years)

Consumer spending per full-time worker

$20,000

Wages & salaries after tax
per full-time worker

$10,000

1900 1902 1904 1906 1908 1910 1912 1914 1916 1918 1920 1922 1924 1926 1928

Source: US Census; US Bureau of Economic Analysis; Historical Statistics of the US; classicalprinciples.com; shaded area denotes *progressive* policies

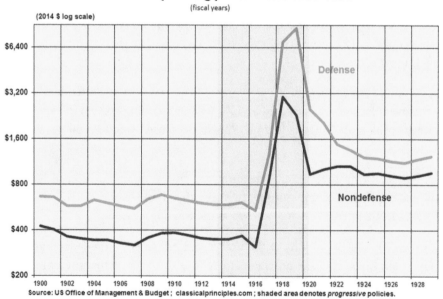

Federal Spending per Worker: 1900-1929

(2014 $ log scale)   (fiscal years)

$6,400

Defense

$3,200

$1,600

$800

Nondefense

$400

$200

1900 1902 1904 1906 1908 1910 1912 1914 1916 1918 1920 1922 1924 1926 1928

Source: US Office of Management & Budget ; classicalprinciples.com ; shaded area denotes *progressive* policies.

CHAPTER 9

The Great Depression: 1929-1940

This would be a great time in the world for some man to come along that knew something. — Will Rogers

The period from 1929 to 1945 corresponds to the most sustained, aggressive shift away from free market, classical principles of any period in the nation's history. It is also one of the most confusing periods in terms of the crosscurrents of shifting economic policies.

In addition to the shift from classical to progressive policies, the period from 1929 to 1940 involved two liquidity crises. A liquidity crisis occurs when there is not enough money in the economy to allow businesses to operate as they normally would. Although the Federal Reserve was created specifically to prevent such crises, it failed to fulfill its mission on two separate occasions during the 1930s.

Our focus here is not on short-term cyclical swings due to changes in the amount of money available to conduct business. Rather, our concern is with the more fundamental policies that either promote or undermine the longer-term creation of wealth. From our perspective, the main point is to show how, after the hiatus of the 1920s, progressive economic policies were reintroduced, first by President Herbert Hoover and then by President Franklin Delano Roosevelt (FDR).

A curious anomaly of the Harding/Coolidge Administrations was Commerce Secretary, Herbert Hoover. Hoover was an engineer who believed an engineer's efficiency could help government guide the economy. As Commerce Secretary he vigorously promoted programs of federal financial assistance to help new homeowners.

Hoover's reliance on government was the exception to the rule during the Harding/Coolidge years. All that would change in March of 1929 when the engineer became President. Hoover's policies brought about an abrupt end to the mostly free market, limited government policies of Calvin Coolidge. Whereas Coolidge had shifted economic power and control from government to individuals, Hoover shifted power and control back to government.

The sharp downward trend in federal spending came to an end in the budget year ending June, 1928 when federal spending increased by 3.5%. The following year federal spending increased by 5.5%, slightly faster than spending in the entire economy. Hoover's first budget beginning in July, 1929 increased federal spending by 6%. This occurred while spending in the entire economy fell by 2%.

Further sharp increases in federal spending in the following years corresponded to a collapse in economic activity. After four years of the Hoover Presidency, real federal spending had increased by over 90% while real output had declined by 24%.

As economic activity collapsed in 1932, Hoover promoted the largest tax increase since 1918. Rates for the lowest paid worker went from 1.5% to 4%. Higher brackets were increased to 60% or more. Tax rates on incomes over $100,000 went from 25% to 56% while the top rate for millionaires, billionaires and corporations went from 25% to 60%.

Hoover also objected to free markets. He associated higher prices and wages with prosperity. As with President Wilson, Hoover successfully persuaded businesses to keep wages higher than market levels. By discouraging businesses from adjusting wages to changing conditions, Hoover's intervention contributed to losses and bankruptcies.

In an attempt to help farmers keep agricultural prices above market levels, Hoover established the Federal Farm Board. The Board moved immediately to encourage more agricultural output, while encouraging farmers to hold on to their crops and wait for higher prices. When farm prices fell, the Farm Board encouraged farmers not to grow crops as a means of raising prices.

In discussing Hoover's farm policy, James Bovard writes, *"In August 1931, the Farm Board urged Southern farmers to destroy every third row of cotton; Southern politicians suggested that farmers instead destroy every third member of the Farm Board."*

In an attempt to protect American jobs and businesses from foreign competition and maintain high prices, Hoover favored a tax on imports. His solution was the infamous Smoot-Hawley tariff. More than 1,000 economists urged Hoover not to sign the tariff bill due to its destructive impact. Hoover ignored the advice. He signed the tariff bill in June of 1930. By 1932 total imports and exports fell to 5% of the economy, half of what they were in 1929.

Hoover completely reversed the classical policies of the 1920s with his increases in government spending, high price and wage policies and a massive tax increase. For the second time its history, the United States had fully embraced the progressive agenda.

In 1932 the public opted for change. In a stroke of incredibly good timing, Roosevelt took the oath of office in the exact month the Hoover recession ended. In his book, *The Midas Paradox,* Scott Sumner argues that FDR's decision to abandon the gold standard immediately ended the nation's liquidity crisis. As a result, between March and August of 1933, industrial production soared by more than 50%. It appeared a sustained recovery was underway. It was not.

FDR's first budget for the fiscal year beginning July, 1934 increased federal spending by 40%. Tax rates also increased dramatically under FDR with increases specifically targeted toward millionaires, billionaires and corporations. By 1938, the top tax rate reached 79%.

In addition to increases in federal spending and tax rates, FDR expanded the government's control over many aspects of the economy. As did Wilson and Hoover, FDR favored government policies to raise prices and wages. FDR signed the National Industrial Recovery Act (NIRA) in June, 1933. The law authorized widespread government control over wages and prices. As with Hoover and Wilson, FDR assumed government efforts to raise wages and prices would produce prosperity.

The NIRA did succeed in raising wages. From 1933 to 1940 real hourly wages and industrial production increased by roughly 40%. In spite of this recovery, the economy remained depressed. The unemployment rate in 1940 was 16%. While real wages had recovered, profits remained depressed. Hence, jobs were not readily available.

In spite of the cyclical recovery from the lows in 1933, massive government intervention into the economy had replaced the nation's once legendary prosperity with widespread poverty.

Wages & Consumer Spending: 1920 to 1945

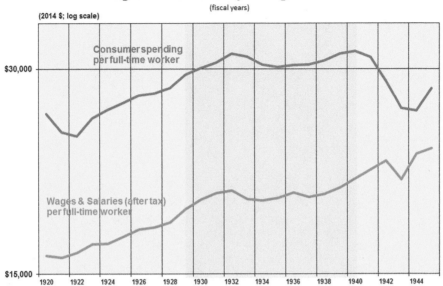

Source: US Bureau of Economic Analysis; Historical Statistics of the US; BLS; classicalprinciples.com; shaded area denotes progressive policies.

Federal Spending per Worker: 1920-1945

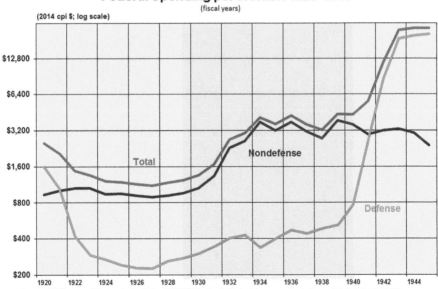

Source: US Bureau of Economic Analysis; OMB; BLS; classicalprinciples.com; shaded area denotes progressive policies.

CHAPTER 10

Restoring Prosperity: 1940-1965

With the war, America was once again ready to become extraordinary.

World War II brought about an end to the Depression. Or did it? Wartime sacrifices are sometimes necessary to ensure a nation's freedom and security. However, wartime prosperity is often an illusion.

At the beginning of 1940, there were about 9 million unemployed US workers. Ten million joined the armed forces during World War II. Demand for workers to supply armaments created jobs for millions more. The result was an explosive growth in output and jobs. By 1945 the unemployment rate was down to 1.5%.

Every economy has the ability to create the illusion of wartime prosperity without resorting to the horrors of war. An authoritarian government can enlist millions into military service, order the production of armaments, and proceed to dump the armaments into the ocean. Under such conditions, the explosive growth in economic output would be similar to what occurred during World War II.

Creating wealth is more than creating jobs and output. Wealth involves the efficient production of things people value. From 1940 to 1945 real consumer spending per *full-time* worker fell by 9%. From this perspective, the period represents an extension of the Depression.

From another perspective, the war years produced a meaningful recovery. Jobs, wages, and prices all soared. As a result, real consumer spending per person increased by 25%. Shortages and rationing were common. Wage and price controls were expanded in an effort to contain inflation.

Just as the war distorted many measures of economic activity, the same is true for the transition back to a peacetime economy. The period following World War II included a major reduction in federal spending, lower tax rates and the deregulation of businesses and markets. By the fall of 1946 most price controls were removed. As in all previous periods, the move back toward free-market, classical principles corresponded to a period of rapid growth and increased prosperity.

The massive shift from wartime to peacetime production from 1945 to 1948 coincided with a 28% rise in consumer spending per full-time worker. These were the first significant increases since 1929. Workers were once again able to buy the things they and their families valued. The Depression was over.

The period from 1940 to 1953 included alternating elements of both classical and progressive policies. Progressive policies were implemented during both World War II and the Korean War and removed after the wars. However, the moves to increase tax rates, federal spending and controls over business and markets were more a reaction to the war than a prescription for somehow improving the economy. The period from 1940 to 1953 is dominated more by the cycles of war and peace than to a commitment to either classical or progressive policies. As a result, these years are not characteristic of either set of policies.

Free-market classical principles and the economy's golden years

The most impressive stage of the postwar recovery occurred from 1953 to 1965. As the period began, price controls from the Korean War expired. To make sure they didn't come back, President Eisenhower abolished the organization responsible for overseeing such controls. There were tax cuts in 1953 and 1954 and federal spending was contained. From 1953 to 1965 federal spending increased by 67%, compared to an increase of 86% in the total economy.

As in previous periods, the combination of a return to free markets, minimal regulation of business, lower tax rates and slower growth in overall federal spending was accompanied by an economic boom. When federal spending grows slower than spending in the rest of the economy, more of the gains from growth go to workers and investors. Between 1953 and 1965 workers' take home pay increased at an average yearly rate of 2.5%. By 1965 average real wages were 33% higher than in 1953.

The slower growth in federal spending was due entirely to a 22% decline in spending for defense. In 1953 the federal defense spending totaled $53 billion and nondefense spending was $19 billion. By 1965, spending on nondefense was $69 billion while defense was $51 billion.

The main source of the increase in nondefense spending was for human services. In a sign of things to come, Social Security payments began to accelerate. By 1965 they accounted for more than half the increase in spending on human services.

In addition, the budget included a major new federal infrastructure project—the Interstate Highway System. This project is one of those rare examples where federal spending was more productive than if the funds had been left in the private sector. The cost of this program was less than $4.5 billion a year, paid for by a tax on gasoline.

There is an important issue to consider concerning tax rates in the 1950s and early 60s. While tax schedules show marginal tax rates as high as 90%, these were not the rates people paid. Extensive studies at the Harris Bank of Chicago used annual IRS *Statistics of Income* reports to identify rates paid by the 70th and 95th percentile of all taxpayers. These studies show the highest rates paid by these upper income households in the 1950s and early 1960s were consistently less than 26%.

The combination of generous deductions and a 25% maximum tax on capital gains meant few, if anyone, actually paid the rates reported in the income tax schedules. For upper income individuals and investors, the boom years of the 1950s and early 60s were periods of relatively low effective tax rates.

The charts below show trends in consumer spending and wages along with federal spending. It's readily apparent how major gains in wages and consumer spending are once again inversely related to the growth rates in overall federal spending. It also was becoming apparent how difficult it could be to contain the growth in federal spending amid the growth in nondefense spending.

The next chapter shows how a dramatic shift to progressive policies brought the nation's golden years of growth to an abrupt end.

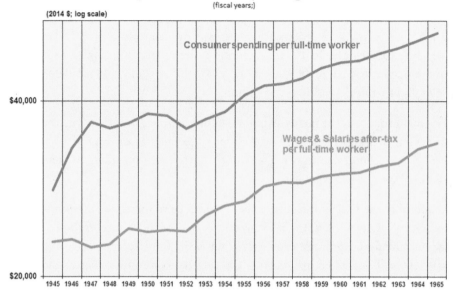

Wages & Consumer Spending: 1945 - 1965

(fiscal years;)

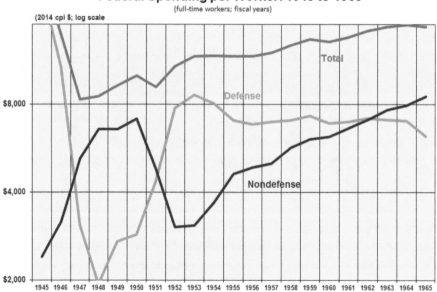

Federal Spending per Worker: 1945 to 1965

(full-time workers; fiscal years)

CHAPTER 11

The Age of Aquarius & the Reagan Recovery: 1965-1988

Our aim is not only to relieve the symptom of poverty, but to cure it and, above all, to prevent it. — President Lyndon Johnson (January, 1964)

One of the great mistakes is to judge policies and programs by their intentions rather than their results. — Milton Friedman (timeless)

The post-World War II expansion came to an end in the late 1960s as the nation's policies shifted away from free-market classical principles. As with his progressive predecessors, President Lyndon Johnson had lofty goals for the federal government. He intended to wield the power of government to eliminate and prevent poverty.

As the classical period came to an end in 1965, tax cuts and modest increases in federal spending contributed to a surge in the economy. These would be the last classical policies for more than a decade.

The first tentative signs of a move back to the progressive agenda actually occurred in 1964 with passage of the Food Stamp Act and Economic Opportunity Act. These were followed in 1965 with the creation of Medicare, Medicaid and the Elementary and Secondary Educational Act. The remainder of the progressive agenda would soon follow.

Federal spending soared in 1966 as Johnson's war on poverty and an escalation in the war in Vietnam produced a 13% increase in the federal budget. From 1965 to 1981, federal spending increased 40% faster than spending in the rest of the economy. Nondefense spending increased almost twice as fast as total spending.

In August, 1971, rising inflationary pressures led Republican President Richard Nixon to declare a freeze on wages and prices. As during earlier periods when government interfered in markets, shortages appeared. Farmers destroyed their animals or failed to ship them to markets rather than lose money at government-controlled prices. Goods began disappearing from the shelves of supermarkets. As shortages increased, the failure of price controls became readily apparent and many were gradually removed.

One price control that remained was on oil. Price controls on oil placed severe limits on oil output. On two separate occasions, in 1973 and again in 1979, the controls contributed to long lines of frustrated drivers waiting for their ration of gasoline.

Tax increases were also prevalent during this period. The tax on capital gains increased from 25% in 1967 to a peak of 49% in 1977. Beginning in 1968, a temporary 10% income surtax was introduced. In 1969, Nixon approved of increases in Social Security taxes as well as an alternative minimum tax targeting the rich.

As in the 1950s, there was a substantial difference between listed tax rates and the rates individuals actually paid. Tax studies using annual IRS *Statistics of Income* reports show the highest effective tax rate for most upper income individuals was 22% in 1965. By 1981 it had increased to a peak rate of 38%.

As with previous moves toward progressive economic policies, there was a significant increase in regulations. From 1965 to 1981, federal regulatory spending went from $1 billion to $7.5 billion. Private spending necessary to comply with federal regulations is estimated to be more than forty times the regulatory budget. Modest moves toward deregulation in the late 1970s were insufficient to overcome these increases. The same is true for tax rates, where a cut in capital gains taxes to 30% in 1978 was mostly offset by inflation pushing taxpayers into sharply higher tax brackets.

By 1979 the economy was in the worst shape since the 1930s. Inflation reached 13% while unemployment was rising toward 7%. Shortages and rationing of gasoline were common. For the first time since the 1930s polls indicated the public lost faith in the economy and in the future.

In the summer of 1979, President Jimmy Carter responded to the nation's economic problems by blaming the public. He said America's problem was a lack of confidence and urged people to join him in adapting to a new age of limits. By telling Americans how they needed to adjust to a new reality, Carter's speech became known as the "malaise speech," a reflection of the nation's economic malaise.

America's third experiment with progressive economic policies left in its wake the same failed economy as the two prior experiments. The government's war on poverty had not only failed to improve the condition of the poor, it ended up reducing living standards for most workers.

In November of 1980 the public rejected the concept of a future with little or no growth. They elected President Ronald Reagan. Reagan, who had studied free-market classical principles at Eureka College in the early 1930s, became a leading advocate for those principles.

Reagan pledged to remove government regulations on individuals and businesses, to restore free markets, to cut tax rates and to reduce the growth in the money supply to control inflation. He also pledged to increase military spending and slow the growth in nondefense spending.

One of Reagan's first moves upon taking office was to end price controls on oil and petroleum products. Not only did this move end gas lines, it actually *lowered* gas prices.

With inflation at double-digits, Reagan supported the Fed's effort to slow the growth in the money supply. This policy led to a recession from 1981 to 1982. By 1983 the inflation rate was down to 3% and the economy was on a strong growth trajectory.

Reagan engineered tax cuts through a hesitant Congress and reduced the growth in federal regulatory spending to half the growth in the economy. Total federal spending, which initially increased amid a military buildup, grew slower than spending in the rest of the economy each year from 1983 to 1989.

For the third time in history, progressive economic policies had been accompanied by poor economic performance. And, for the third time, a reversal of such policies was followed by significant increases in workers' take-home pay and consumer spending.

In spite of the success of this shift in policies, by the late 1980s, elements of the progressive agenda were about to return.

Wages and Consumer Spending: 1965 to 1988
(fiscal years)

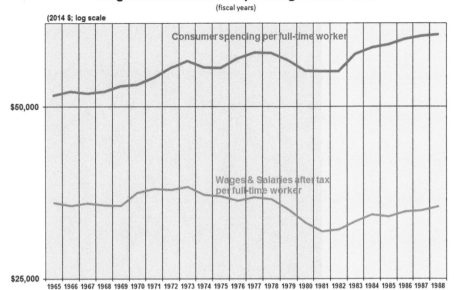

Source: US Bureau of Economic Analysis; BLS; classicalprinciples.com ; shaded area represents *progressive* policies

Federal Spending per Worker: 1965-1988
(fiscal years)

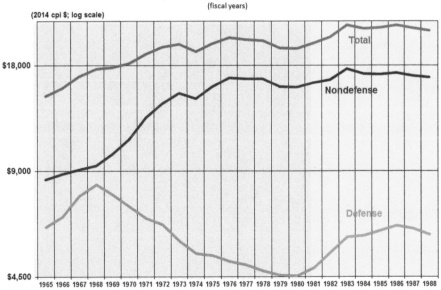

Source: US Bureau of Economic Analysis; OMB; BLS; classicalprinciples.com; shaded area reflects *progressive* policies

CHAPTER 12

At the Dawn of the 21st Century

Insanity: doing the same thing over and over again and expecting different results.
— Albert Einstein

From the late 1980s to the mid-1990s economic policies once again shifted away from free-market classical principles. One of the policies contributing to this shift was the Tax Reform Act of 1986. The Act, signed by President Reagan, took effect in 1987 and 1988.

In previous chapters we noted how successful tax cuts provided savers and investors with the incentives and funds needed to increase wealth. The 1986 tax changes were different. They included a combination of lower tax rates to help boost wealth and higher tax rates to offset the expected revenue loss from the tax cuts.

While the 1986 Act reduced the top tax rates for some individuals, it increased the tax burdens for others, particularly savers, investors and businesses. It did so by raising the capital gains tax from 20% to 28%, increasing corporate tax rates, closing various loopholes and by extending depreciation allowances for housing and commercial real estate.

The complex relationship between the tax system and economic activity means changes in tax laws can have unintended consequences. This occurred with the 1986 Act. The combination of closing loopholes and a higher tax on capital gains raised the *effective* tax rate for certain middle and upper middle income tax payers. In addition, extending depreciation allowances reduced the value of certain real estate assets. A decline in the value of these assets contributed to a savings and loan (S&L) industry crisis. A Federal Deposit Insurance Corporation review of the impact on the S&L industry from 1986-95 concluded there were 1,043 thrift failures costing taxpayers and the industry approximately $150 billion.

When the economy slowed, policymakers chose to raise taxes again. In 1990 President George H.W. Bush was persuaded to increase the top tax rate on individuals to 31%. In 1993, President Bill Clinton followed with a variety of tax increases designed to target the rich. Among these were increases in the top individual tax rate to 39.6% and an increase in the capital gains tax for business.

Nondefense federal spending soared from 1988 to 1995. However, total federal spending increased only slightly more than spending in the rest of the economy. Total federal spending was contained when the collapse of the Soviet Union led to major cuts in the defense budget. Government regulations also increased during this period with the federal regulatory budget increasing more than twice as fast as in the 1981 to 1988 period.

As with earlier policy shifts away from free-market classical principles, the impact from slower economic growth was particularly hard on workers. In the seven years from 1988 to 1995 wages fell by 3%. The Reagan recovery had stalled.

By 1995, a stagnant economy contributed to voters placing Republicans in charge of both Houses of Congress. The leadership pledged to slow the growth in federal spending, reduce tax rates and cut government regulations. This is one of those rare episodes in history when Republicans actually drove the budget debate. When President Clinton agreed to go along, the objectives were met. As a result, the period from 1995 to 2004 represents a policy shift back toward a free-market classical agenda.

From 1995 to 2004, federal spending grew 25% less than spending in the rest of the economy. Tax cuts in 1997 reduced the tax burden on workers and investors while lowering the capital gains tax to 20%. There was another series of tax cuts beginning in 2001. These cuts lowered the top tax bracket to 35% and the maximum capital gains tax to 15%.

With slower growth in federal spending and tax cuts for investors and workers, the economy grew rapidly. From 1995 to 2004 average worker take-home pay increased by 19% while consumer spending per worker rose by 18%. The tax cuts from 2001 to 2004 were consistent with the final stage of the economy's recovery. As this period was ending, federal spending accelerated amid both a response to the terrorist attacks of 9/11 and an expansion in government programs.

From 2004 to 2015 the nation experienced its fifth move in the direction of the progressive policy agenda. This period included an economic boom, a financial crisis, a steep recession and a recovery. Our focus is not on these cyclical ups and downs, all of which were driven by the Federal Reserve's monetary policy. As with earlier periods, our focus is on the longer-term, secular trends in the economy.

From 2004 to 2015, federal spending increased by 40% more than spending in the rest of the economy. This was due to a surge in nondefense spending. In spite of wars in Iraq and Afghanistan, military spending increased much less than spending in the rest of the economy.

In addition to major increases in federal spending, massive new regulatory burdens were placed on the economy. These burdens consisted of new government controls over banking, healthcare and energy.

Tax rates were also increased with an emphasis on taxing the rich. In 2013 the highest tax on capital gains went from 15% to 20% and the top effective individual tax rate increased to more than 40%. In addition, government increasingly used the federal budget to subsidize politically-favored businesses.

The shift in economic policies took its toll on the economy. Average worker take-home pay declined slightly, while consumer spending per worker increased by only 0.7% a year. Higher payroll taxes and health insurance mandates raised the costs of hiring workers, particularly full-time workers.

As with previous periods dominated by progressive policies, there was a widespread belief the nation's best days were over and future generations would have to adjust to lower living standards.

Wages & Consumer Spending: 1981 to 2015

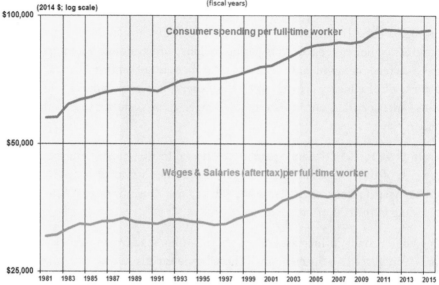

Source: US Bureau of Economic Analysis; BLS;; classicalprinciples.com; shaded areas denote *progressive* policies

Federal Spending per Worker: 1981-2015

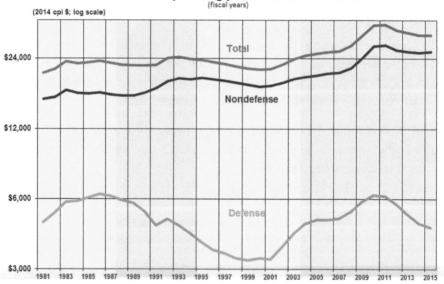

Source: US Bureau of Economic Analysis; OMB; BLS; classicalprinciples.com; shaded areas denote progressive policies

This chapter completes our historical analysis of the impact of two distinct sets of economic policies from 1900-2015. The next chapter summarizes the economy's performance during the different policy agendas and discusses their implications for the future.

CHAPTER 13

Summarizing the US Experience

All theory is against freedom of the will; all experience for it.
— Samuel Johnson

The preceding chapters presented historical details for two distinct sets of policies. Beginning in 1900, we identified five separate periods, consisting of fifty years, when economic policies were moving primarily in the direction of the free-market classical policy agenda. We also identified five alternative periods consisting of fifty-two years when policies were moving primarily in the direction of the progressive policy agenda. The remaining years, from 1940-53 were dominated by cycles of war and peace. They are too unusual to place in either policy category.

For each of these periods we presented charts showing two measures of economic activity—real take-home wages per full-time worker and real consumer spending per full-time worker. For short-hand we'll refer to these as wages and consumer spending. The table below summarizes the performance of these measures in terms of average annual changes.

	1900	Classical	Progressive	1940-53
Wages	1.0%	2.1%	-0.1%	1.6%
Consumer Spending	1.5%	2.2%	1.0%	1.2%

We begin with their average performance over the entire period and then compare it to the average performance during each period of alternative policies. The growth in wages during the fifty years when policies moved in the direction of free-market classical principles accounts for 87% of the entire growth in wages since 1900. The remaining increase in wages occurred during the 1940-53 period. There was *no increase* in wages over the fifty-two years when policies moved in the direction of the progressive agenda.

It can be instructive to compare the *actual growth* in wages to what the growth might have been if either classical or progressive policies had prevailed over the entire period. Our simulation uses only growth rates during classical periods to generate a series of hypothetical wages implied by classical policies. Similarly, we use only growth rates during progressive periods to generate hypothetical wages implied by progressive policies. Both simulations use actual growth rates for 1940-53, the period when policies were neither consistently classical nor progressive.

The actual performance of wages from 1900-2015 produced an average wage of approximately $38,000 in 2015. The classical simulation produces an average wage in 2015 of $114,500, about three times the actual wage. The progressive simulation produces an average wage in 2015 of $20,200. All of the increase in wages in the progressive simulation is due to the use of actual growth rates for the war years 1940-53. Using only the growth rates from the 52 years of progressive policies produces an average wage in 2015 of $15,200, slightly below the average wage in 1913.

US Wages: Actual & Alernative Policies
(fiscal years)

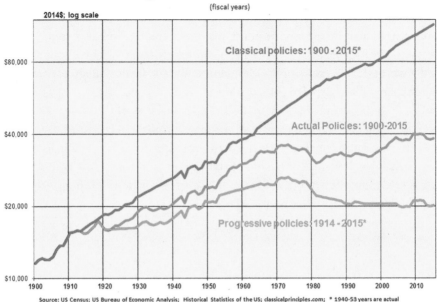

Source: US Census; US Bureau of Economic Analysis; Historical Statistics of the US; classicalprinciples.com; * 1940-53 years are actual

It is impossible to relive the past century to observe what wages could have been had the nation consistently applied either classical or progressive policies. However, as we will see in the following chapters, what is a hypothetical for the US is a reality in other countries.

Many countries in the world never pursued free-market classical policies. The inability of these countries to experience any significant improvement in living standards is similar to the US experience during periods dominated by progressive policies.

In contrast, countries consistently applying free-market classical principles have experienced the type of extraordinary performance depicted in our hypothetical example for the US. For example, Singapore's output per person in 1965 was 30% less than in the US. After half a century of a steady dose of free-market classical principles, Singapore's output per person in 2015 was 50% more than in the US.

The implication of our analysis should be clear. By applying free-market classical principles from its birth, the US at the dawn of the 20th century had become world's most prosperous economy. Since 1913, whenever the US deviated from its founding principles, its economy behaved in a manner similar to what is found in the world's poorest nations.

Having examined the economic policy history of the US, the next step is to examine the impact classical policies have had on economies throughout the rest of the world. Ideally, it would be desirable to have a detailed analysis of various policy changes and detailed information on workers' wages as we have for the United States. A detailed policy analysis of the countries of the world is well beyond the scope of this book. Instead, for international comparisons, the Fraser Institute's measures of economic freedom provide a proxy for free market classical principles. For measuring living standards we use the most conventional measure available for international comparisons—a nation's output per person based on purchasing power parity (PPP).

CHAPTER 14

Wealth in the Western Offshoots

What do I think of Western civilization? I think it would be a very good idea.
– Mahatma Gandhi

For all international comparisons, we follow Angus Maddison's approach of using output per person adjusted for purchasing power parity as our measure of general well-being or wealth. In his analysis of long-term global growth, Maddison refers to the United States, Canada, Australia and New Zealand as "Western Offshoots." He observes how, historically, this group had experienced much more rapid growth than Western Europe.

For the most part, this has continued. The Fraser Institute's measures of economic freedom indicate how the United States had the highest level of economic freedom of all the Western Offshoots until 1995. The United States also consistently has had the highest level of wealth among the Offshoots.

Canada, which had the second highest level of economic freedom prior to the 1990s, has mostly had the second highest level of wealth among this group. New Zealand, which traditionally had the lowest level of economic freedom, consistently had the lowest level of wealth among the group.

As we will see in subsequent chapters, the type of sustained, high degree of economic freedom, such as we saw in the United States, has consistently been associated with a high level of wealth. Even if the degree of economic freedom moderates, a high level of wealth can be maintained. This is because high levels of wealth over time are associated with a buildup of key assets, such as infrastructure, buildings and technological expertise. The greater amounts of these assets enable individuals to generate higher levels of wealth than those in countries with fewer such assets.

Also, as we saw in the United States and as we will see in other countries, while a major change in a country's economic freedom tends to be directly associated with a change in the nation's economic performance, these changes are seldom instantaneous. As we saw in the charts for the United States, there is often a lag between a major change in economic freedom and the subsequent change in economic performance.

Among the Western Offshoots, the country with the greatest recent change in economic freedom is New Zealand. In the decade from 1985 to 1995, New Zealand's economic freedom measure went from being the lowest among the Western Offshoots to being the highest. The change was associated with a major improvement in New Zealand's wealth. In the two decades ending in 2015, New Zealand's wealth increased by 39%. This was *more than four times* the increase experienced during the previous two decades.

Australia had a similar development. Although the nation's economic freedom score did not increase as dramatically as did New Zealand's, Australia's increase started from a higher level. Hence, Australia had sufficiently greater assets to maintain a higher level of wealth. In the two decades ending in 2015, Australia's wealth increased 43%, more than double the increase in the previous two decades. Australia's rapid increase enabled it to pass Canada. By 2015, Australia was the second wealthiest of the Western Offshoots.

Although Canada's economic freedom measure remains high, there has been little change since 1990. This lack of improvement has been associated with the slowest increase in wealth among this group. In the two decades ending in 2015, Canada's wealth increased by 33%, about three times the increase in the previous two decades. While impressive by most standards, the increase in wealth in both Canada and the United States has been the slowest among the Western Offshoots in the twenty years ending in 2015.

Unfortunately, all of the Western Offshoots have experienced a decline in economic freedom since the turn of the century. The United States has fallen from the freest of the four countries in 1990 to the least free since 2005. In spite of this decline, the United States has maintained its position as the wealthiest of the

Western Offshoots. Its relative position has been helped by a more substantial level of assets and by the decline in freedom for the rest of this group.

High degrees of economic freedom have helped these Western Offshoots maintain high levels of wealth. However, the recent erosion in economic freedom has been followed by slower growth in each country. Given the lags normally associated with changes in economic freedom, it's likely all of the Western Offshoots will continue to experience slow growth in subsequent years.

Economic Freedom: Western Offshoots

Source: Fraser Institute; Economic Freedom of the World, 2016 Annual Report; (5 year intervals until 2000)

Output per Person: Western Offshoots

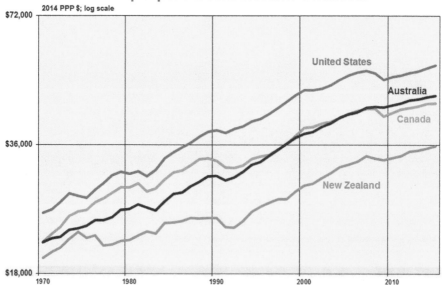

Source: Angus Maddison, The World Economy; IMF, World Economic Outlook Database, April 2016; classicalprinciples.com

CHAPTER 15

Economic Freedom in Europe

Europe is not based on a common language, culture and values... Europe is the result of plans. It is in fact, a classic utopian project, a monument to the vanity of intellectuals, a programme whose inevitable destiny is failure; only the scale of the final damage done is in doubt. — Margaret Thatcher

Those who favor giving more power and control to government often point to the success of various European countries with large government sectors. This chapter begins by comparing the wealthiest of European economies to the United States. We then show how trends in economic freedom and wealth have been related among Europe's largest economies.

Before comparing Europe to the US, it's important to recall how US policies have been moving toward a greater reliance on government. An example of such a move has been the increase in US government spending as a percent the economy from 29% in 2000 to 36% in 2015. From this perspective, US policies have moved significantly toward the European model.

Only countries with at least several million people are included in our analysis. Luxembourg, a European country with less than 600,000 people, is often cited as the wealthiest non-oil producing country in the world with output per person of almost $100,000. Even if Luxembourg had a larger population, the country is not a useful model for insights on creating wealth. Luxembourg is a tax haven and private banking center. Much of its extraordinary wealth appears to be related more to facilitating the transfer and protection of wealth than to its creation.

In 2015, Europe's three wealthiest countries were Norway, Switzerland and Ireland. Here's a brief summary of each.

Norway is the wealthiest country in Europe. In 2015, its output per person amounted to almost $68,000. A significant part of Norway's "wealth" is due to its extensive natural resources. The European Commission reports oil and gas alone account for 22% of Norway's output. With only 5 million people, Norway's "wealth" appears closely related to its abundance of natural resources.

Norway's government sector is relatively large when compared to the US, but relatively small when compared to most other European countries. Government spending in Norway has tended to be 40% to 45% of the economy's output. This is closer to that of Germany and Spain than to the 50% or higher levels in most other European countries.

There is a significant spread between Norway's $68,000 of output per person and its neighbors. The next wealthiest Scandinavian country is Sweden with $48,000. Sweden's efficiency is typical of much of the rest of Europe where output per person is in the $40,000 to $50,000 vicinity. The distinguishing factor in Norway's wealth, from most of the rest of Europe, appears to be its oil and gas reserves. In his book, *Debunking Utopia: Exposing the Myth of Nordic Socialism*, Swedish analyst Nima Sanandaji provides extensive evidence on the failure of socialism in the Scandinavian countries.

Switzerland was Europe's next wealthiest nation in 2015. Unlike Norway, its economy doesn't benefit from natural resources. Switzerland is rated the fourth most economically free country in the world. Its government sector is relatively small, particularly for Europe. In 2015 government spending amounted to about a third of the country's output, slightly below the level in the US. The country's economic success appears directly related to its policies. These policies include a relatively small government sector, minimal government regulations and minimal barriers to free markets. It is the exception to the more common European model which relies on a large government sector and more regulations.

Ireland was the third wealthiest country in Europe in 2015. Its government share of the economy was 34%, slightly above Switzerland but also below the United States. The relationship between Ireland's growth and prosperity appears similar to the experience we found in the United States.

From 1990 to 2015 Ireland experienced one of the greatest increases in wealth of any nation. As in the United States, Ireland's major increase in growth corresponded to those years where it limited its government spending. From 1985 to

2005 government spending in Ireland increased by half the increase in spending in the rest of the economy.

The financial crisis in 2008-09 hit Ireland's economy hard. Real output fell by 7.5%. As with most countries, the economic collapse led to a sharp increase in government spending. Unlike most countries, Ireland responded to the crisis with severe cuts in government spending. From its peak in 2010 to 2015 Ireland cut government spending by 32%. Unlike the rest of Europe, Ireland's economy soared. By 2015, the nation's wealth rebounded to match that in the US.

Ireland's success was not simply a function of reducing the size and power of its government. The increase corresponded to a significant increase in the nation's economic freedom. Ireland is rated as the 8th most economically free country in the world. Hence, Ireland's wealth appears directly related to the adoption of free-market classical policies.

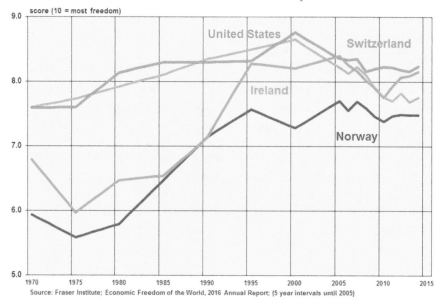

Economic Freedom: The US & Europe's Wealthiest

score (10 = most freedom)

United States

Switzerland

Ireland

Norway

Source: Fraser Institute; Economic Freedom of the World, 2016 Annual Report; (5 year intervals until 2005)

Output per Person: The US & Europe's Wealthiest

2014 PPP $: log scale

Norway

Switzerland

Ireland

United States

Source: Angus Maddison, The World Economy; International Monetary Fund; World Economic Database, April, 2016; classicalprinciples.com

Germany, France and the United Kingdom are the three largest economies in the European Union (EU) in terms of total output. In 2015, the three accounted for 48% of the EU's output. As we have found with so many other nations, there is often a direct relationship between economic freedom and wealth in these countries.

In the early 1970s, Germany had the greatest economic freedom of this group. The UK had the least. Since the mid-1970s, the UK has experience the greatest improvement in economic freedom. In 1980, wealth in the UK was more than 20% below that in Germany. Reforms led by Margaret Thatcher produced substantial gains in economic freedom, which peaked in 2000. By 2005, wealth in the UK improved to within 5% of Germany. With the decline in UK's freedom since 2000, the UK's wealth has dipped to 12% below that of Germany.

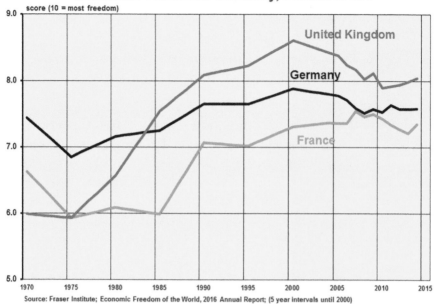

Source: Fraser Institute; Economic Freedom of the World, 2016 Annual Report; (5 year intervals until 2000)

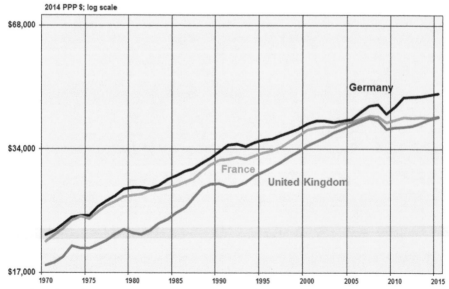

Source: Angus Maddison, The World Economy; IMF, World Economic Outlook Database, April 2016; classicalprinciples.com

In contrast to the higher levels of freedom in the UK, France has almost consistently had the least amount of economic freedom of this group. France has also experienced the slowest increase in wealth of the three. In the 1970s, wealth in France was on par with Germany. By 2015, France's wealth was 12% below Germany. Also in the 1970's, France's wealth was as much as 25% above that in the UK. With its increase in economic freedom, the UK was able to pull even with France.

As a whole, Europe is not an economically healthy area. Twenty-five years ago, IMF estimates show the EU produced 30% of the world's output. In 2015, the share was down to 17%. We noted how the most successful countries in Europe were those with both more economic freedom and smaller government sectors. The same is true for the three largest countries.

France, the slowest growing of the three has the largest government sector. In France, government spending accounts for 57% of its output. In Germany government spending is 44% of output, three percentage points below the EU average. At 40%, the UK has the smallest government share of these three countries. This reaffirms a general tendency we find in many countries. Beyond a certain level, the more the government's share of output increases, the more it undermines a nation's wealth.

The idea that European countries with large bureaucratic government sectors are examples of highly successful economies is not supported by conventional measures of success. When comparing the creation of wealth, the evidence indicates the most successful European nations are those with smaller government sectors and greater economic freedom.

There should be no mystery regarding most of Europe's economic stagnation at the beginning of the 21st century. Economic stagnation is a normal occurrence when policies move away from free-market classical principles. The results are much different when countries move in the opposite direction, as we will now see with Hong Kong and Singapore.

CHAPTER 16

Economic Freedom in Hong Kong & Singapore

Freedom lies in being bold. — Robert Frost

In the real world, no country faithfully adheres to free-market classical principles. Political pressures to expand government power are usually intense. As a result, there are only degrees of freedom. The two nations widely recognized for possessing the highest degrees of economic freedom in the world are Hong Kong and Singapore.

They are each small countries in terms of both size and population. Hong Kong, the larger of the two, is a third the size of Rhode Island and has only 7 million people. Singapore is slightly smaller with slightly fewer people. Neither country is blessed with natural resources. In the middle of the 20th century, both were poor. Each had to earn its wealth.

In previous chapters we noted how the United States has shifted policies toward and away from free-market, classical principles. In contrast, Hong Kong and Singapore have had a fairly consistent set of policies. Policymakers and citizens in both countries take pride in being recognized as the freest economies in the world.

Elements of economic freedom include a moderate size of government, low tax rates and various other policies related to ease of doing business and free markets. From this perspective, policies in Hong Kong and Singapore stand out from policies throughout most of the rest of the world. This is also true for their economic performance.

In terms of government spending, both countries have very limited government sectors. Total government spending is roughly 20% of each country's output. Prior to the late 1990s, when Hong Kong's growth was often as fast as Singapore's growth, government spending was less than 15% of the nation's output.

As for taxes, instead of vilifying the rich, tax policies in Hong Kong and Singapore are designed to help individuals and businesses succeed and become rich. Hong Kong is often considered the most tax- friendly country in the world. The maximum tax rate for individuals is 15%, and the maximum tax on profits is 16.5%. Numerous deductions and allowances further reduce the actual rates.

Singapore's top tax rates are 20% on individuals and 17% on profits. There is also a 7% tax on goods and services. Neither country taxes capital gains.

As for specific policies, each country takes pride in promoting free markets. Each has almost totally free trade, minimal regulations of businesses, a strong legal system and strong protection of individual property rights.

Consistent with their free market philosophy, social programs in both Singapore and Hong Kong have been limited to helping those unable to help themselves. Welfare is discouraged for those who are able to help themselves. Both countries have imposed mandatory retirement accounts. These force workers to place a portion of their earnings into personal retirement accounts. Although the funds are the property of the worker, there are limits on how and when the funds can be used and on how the earnings can be invested.

In spite of the similarities, there are unique differences in each approach. In Hong Kong, workers and their employers must each contribute 5% of wages into a government-controlled retirement fund. In Singapore, workers must contribute 20% of their wages to a government controlled fund while employers contribute an additional 17%. Hence, Singapore's workers are forced to save 37% of their compensation. This is in addition to paying an income tax and a 7% goods and services tax.

Singapore's retirement system was created in 1955 and, over time, the amount of funds has expanded dramatically. As workers' assets have grown, portions of these funds have been allocated for housing and for healthcare, in a manner similar to Health Savings Accounts (HSAs) in the United States.

The World Bank estimates Singapore's healthcare costs per person were less than $3,000 in 2014. This compares to over $9,000 in the US. There are at least two reasons for the difference. First, Singapore's workers shop carefully since the money they spend on healthcare is their own money. Pilot studies in the US show HSAs cut healthcare costs in half. Second, healthcare in Singapore is based primarily on free market competitive pressures. Such pressures also tend to cut costs in half.

By forcing workers to save a very large portion of their salary, Singapore's system generates a huge surplus of funds for investments. As a result, the power of compound interest works to expand investments and promote wealth. While this is likely a key reason Singapore's wealth has passed so many other countries, forced saving severely limits the freedom workers' have over their earnings.

While Hong Kong usually receives the highest score for economic freedom, Singapore is the clear winner in terms of growth. In 2015, Singapore's output per person was just over $84,000 while Hong Kong was more comparable to the US at $56,700.

As in the US, the wealthier a country becomes, the greater the gap between those who are financially successful and those who are not. This inequality tends to produce political pressures to tax success and redistribute the income to those who have less.

These same pressures are emerging in both Singapore and Hong Kong. Both countries have begun to expand social welfare programs. In 2011, Hong Kong abandoned a part of its free-market tradition by instituting a government-mandated minimum wage. In 2015, Singapore began mandating a minimum wage for certain workers. Beginning in 2017 Singapore will introduce a more progressive tax system raising its maximum rate from 20% to 22% and redistributing income to those in need.

Both Singapore and Hong Kong still retain most of their free-market principles. It will be instructive to see the extent to which they are able to increase their wealth as policies shift from those designed to create wealth to those aimed more at redistributing it.

Economic Freedom: Hong Kong, Singapore & US

Source: Fraser Institute; Economic Freedom of the World, 2016 Annual Report; (chin-link data 5 year intervals until 2000)

Output per Person: Hong Kong, Singapore & US

Source: Angus Maddison, The World Economy; IMF, World Economic Outlook Database, April 2016; classicalprinciples.com

CHAPTER 17

China's Classical "Miracle"

These guys got it right. These are the policies we will adopt. It will take time, but China will be the most powerful economy in the world. — Deng Xiaoping, 1981

Angus Maddison estimates China produced roughly one-third of the world's output in the early 19th century. If so, Chain was by far the largest economy in the world. In the years that followed, China turned inward ignoring both trade and contact with rest of the world. By 1950, China was one of the poorest nations in the world. Output per person was half that of Africa. With 22% of the world's people, it produced only 4.5% of the world's output. Millions of its people were starving.

Deng Xiaoping took over as the head of China in 1978. He was intrigued by free-market classical principles. Upon taking power, his first move was to introduce elements of a market economy into agriculture. Impressive gains in agricultural output convinced him that extending these policies to other parts of the Chinese economy would restore China to its once prominent position as the world's largest economy.

In 1981, my friend and mentor Beryl Sprinkel visited China as a member of President Reagan's Administration. Beryl was thrilled to find the bookshelves of every Chinese official were lined with classical economics textbooks. These were the individuals Deng referred to in the quote above.

Beryl agreed with Deng's bold prediction, but he cautioned, "Under your plans some people will become very rich while others will not be rich. The inequality of incomes will conflict with China's goal of achieving equality."

Deng replied, "Yes, but the poor will be much better off."

It took China only 33 years to realize Deng's bold prediction. Estimates comparing economic output among nations show China surpassed the US in 2014 to become the largest economy in the world. The outcome testifies to the powerful impact free-market policies can have when applied to even the poorest of countries.

China's move toward classical principles was one of the most dramatic policy shifts in history. Every aspect of China's economy had been under the control of the government. The complete lack of freedom had crushed people's initiative and destroyed their ability to generate wealth.

In the early stages of China's free market reforms, government spending grew much slower than spending in the rest of the economy. From 1982 to 1996, increases in government spending averaged 14% a year, while spending in the rest of the economy averaged 20% a year. In 1996, government spending amounted to only 11% of the economy's total output. Tax rates were also extremely low with government revenues amounting to only 10% of the economy's output.

Beginning in the late 1990s, China embarked on a major policy change, one that involved dramatic increases in government spending. From 1996 to 2007 government spending increased by 18% a year, five percentage points faster than spending in the rest of the economy. In spite of this surge, by 2007 government spending still accounted for only 18% of the nation's output.

In other countries we have seen how growth tends to slow when government spending increases faster than spending in the rest of the economy. In China there was only a modest slowdown in growth, from 11% a year to 10%.

There are two reasons China's growth remained rapid while its government sector increased. For one, China's policies continued to move aggressively to restore free markets. Numerous government controls over markets and trade were removed. In addition, much of the increase in government spending went to build infrastructure—roads, ports, railways, airports, power plants and buildings. From 1998 to 2008 real spending on construction increased 16% a year.

All government spending is not the same. We noted in an earlier chapter how government spending can raise a nation's wealth if the funds are used more productively than if they had been left in the hands of the private sector. For example, this can occur when public funds are spent to provide safety, enhance the rule of law or for certain essential infrastructure projects.

China's rapid growth in government spending prior to 2008 may have contributed to increasing its wealth. However, its response to the 2008 financial crisis appears to be an example of inefficient spending. From 2007 to 2015 government spending increased more than twice as fast as spending in the rest of the economy. By 2015 government spending had risen to 32% of the economy's output.

At first, the surge in government spending appeared to work. China maintained its real growth rate at 10% a year. In retrospect, much of the surge in government spending appears to have been unproductive. It led to an excess of both manufacturing capacity and housing. By the end of the period, China's reported growth rate was down to around 6%.

In spite of its success in becoming the largest economy in the world, China is not a wealthy country. In 2015, China's output per person was $14,100. This places the Chinese people approximately in the middle of the world in terms of living standards, well below the $56,000 in the US. Nonetheless, from its low starting point in 1980, the Chinese have been rapidly closing the gap between their living standards and those in other developed countries.

One thing China has failed to do is devolve power from government to individuals. Unlike Singapore and Hong Kong, China's social insurance program resembles that in the United States. Individual contribution rates are high and the funds are then spent to support retirees and other government programs. As a result, the retirement funds are not available for investments. As in the United States, the failure to save and invest these funds undermines the creation of wealth.

Although China continues to deregulate various aspects of its economy, its measure of economic freedom remains below that of most other major countries. Both the Fraser Institute and Heritage Foundation place China's score well below the average of other countries. Given the relationship between economic freedom and wealth, China has a long way to go before being classified as a wealthy nation.

Economic Freedom Scores: US & China

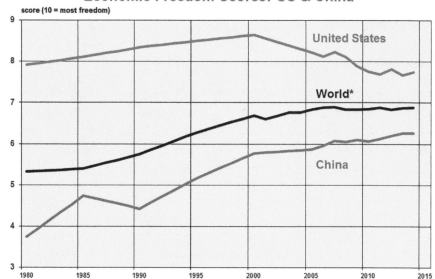

Source: Fraser Institute; Economic Freedom of the World, 2016 Annual Report; (5 year intervals until 2000);
*average of 104 countres with scores since 1980.

Output per Person: United States & China

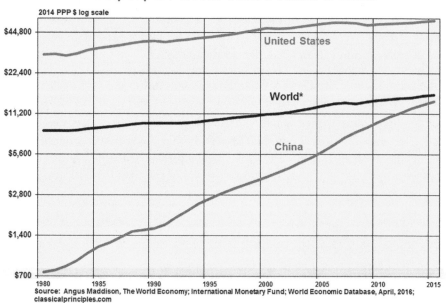

Source: Angus Maddison, The World Economy; International Monetary Fund; World Economic Database, April, 2016;
classicalprinciples.com

CHAPTER 18

India Follows China

And our nation, though it has no drinking water, electricity, sewage system, public transportation, sense of hygiene, discipline, courtesy, or punctuality, does have entrepreneurs. — Aravind Adiga, Indian author

India, with 1.2 billion people, is the second most populous nation in the world. As with China, its legacy of extensive government controls produced abject poverty for hundreds of millions of its people.

After its independence from Britain in 1947, India's leaders blamed colonial exploitation for the country's problems. The leaders turned the country inward, away from world trade. Its leaders were educated in England, where socialism had become popular. The nation's first prime minister referred to capitalism and profit as "bad words." India's political leaders were also enamored with communism and its commitment to a goal of economic equality.

Communism is the polar opposite of economic freedom and free-market classical principles. Whereas socialism refers to government ownership or control of key companies and industries, communism extends government control to all markets, trade and the allocation of resources. Both isms rely extensively on government bureaucrats to run the economy.

India's version of socialism included many of the elements of communism. In the 1950s India nationalized a wide range of industries. It adopted restrictions on international trade, controlled financial markets and adopted an elaborate bureaucracy where numerous government agencies had to approve and regulate every business decision. As with China and the Soviet Union, such controls created a humanitarian disaster.

In 1980 the world's average per capita wealth was estimated to be 73% below that in the US. India's per capita wealth was 77% *below* the world average. At that time, the only major country where people were worse off than India was China, where output per person was 91% below the world average. The abject poverty and widespread starvation in both countries provides testimony to the complete failure of government-controlled economies. Even after China abandoned communism and experienced explosive growth, India held on to its socialist legacy.

A turning point came in 1991 amid a debt crisis, which left the nation's foreign exchange reserves depleted. India faced a major collapse from its already low level of economic activity. As a condition for receiving international aid, the International Monetary Fund required India to move toward a free market economy. In response, India removed its most restrictive requirements for business decisions, cut taxes, sharply reduced its tariffs and opened its markets to foreign investments.

As government controls over the economy eased, growth accelerated. India's real growth in the 1980s averaged 5% a year. It increased to 6% in the 1990s and to 7.5% from 2005 to 2015.

The increase in growth associated with moves toward freer markets in both India and China produced a significant reduction in world poverty. The World Bank estimates that more than a billion and a half people moved out of conditions of abject poverty between 1990 and 2014. With more than a third of the world's population between them, the changes in India and China were responsible for most of this reduction in worldwide poverty.

In two important ways, China and India have taken separate paths to development. The first relates to demographics. In the late 1970s, China's government was able to initiate a one-child policy designed to limit the growth in its population. With China's authoritarian power, its policy took effect. A similar proposal to control India's population through forced sterilization was undertaken in the 1970s, but elements of the program were defeated when a public outcry prevented the policy from taking effect. Unlike China, India's democracy prevented a more dramatic approach to population control.

China's recent population growth is down to only 0.5% a year and its population will soon be declining. In contrast, with fewer limits on its population, India has a young and growing workforce prepared to contribute to the nation's future growth. However, the faster population growth in India makes it more difficult to increase its wealth, measured as output per person.

While the power of China's authoritarian government has created longer-term demographic problems, it has also contributed to a country with world-class buildings, ports, airports, state of the art businesses and high-speed rail lines. An authoritarian government has the power to direct 40% of a country's output toward investments and the results can be impressive.

In a democracy such as India, political pressures often influence public spending. The amount of output spent on investment tends to be only about half as much as in China. As a result, India's infrastructure reflects the poorer country it is.

Recently, India has embarked on a program to improve its infrastructure. It plans to rely on the private sector for roughly half of its infrastructure spending. While relying on the private sector can delay projects, it can also help to avoid wasteful, nonproductive government projects such as those found in China.

Some have referred to rapid growth in both India and China as economic "miracles." They are not miracles. The high growth rates are similar to what we see in any other poor country when policies shift from extensive government controls to greater economic freedom.

In spite of impressive economic gains in growth in India and China, output per person is below the world average in both countries. While both have changed their economic policies in the direction of free-market classical principles, neither is classified as a free economy. In terms of economic freedom, both countries are below the world average.

Both India and China have a great opportunity for further gains in wealth if policymakers continue to move policies in the direction of more economic freedom. While China has a head start over India in creating a wealthier country, India's potential future growth is even greater. With a young and energetic workforce and a rapidly growing private sector, India has the potential to generate higher growth rates well into the future.

Economic Freedom: India & China

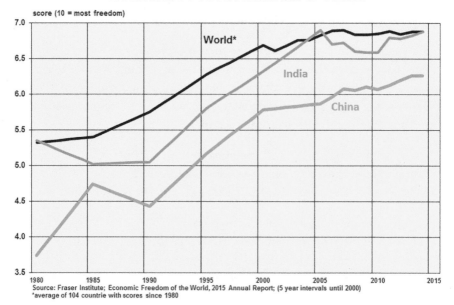

score (10 = most freedom)

Source: Fraser Institute; Economic Freedom of the World, 2015 Annual Report; (5 year intervals until 2000)
*average of 104 countrie with scores since 1980

Output per Person: India & China

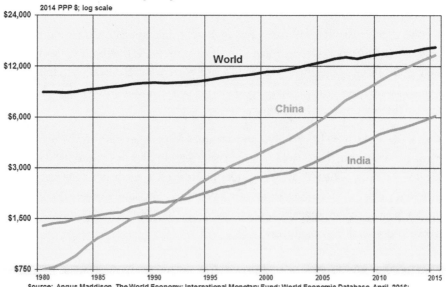

2014 PPP $; log scale

Source: Angus Maddison, The World Economy; International Monetary Fund; World Economic Database, April, 2016;
classicalprinciples.com

CHAPTER 19

Russia: Haunted by its History

For us in Russia, communism is a dead dog, while, for many people in the West,

it is still a living lion. — Aleksandr Solzhenitsyn

In terms of natural resources, Russia may be the richest country in the world. The World Bank estimates that rents from the country's natural resources make up 16% of the nation's output. Some estimates suggest the country might contain 30% of the world's natural resources.

In 2015 Russia was the world's sixth largest economy, producing 3.3% of the world's output. Given its size and resources, Russia's citizens should be among the wealthiest in the world. They are not. Output per person in 2015 was $25,400, less than half that of the United States. Moreover, Russia's output per person was below that in the Czech Republic, Slovenia, the Slovak Republic, Estonia, Lithuania, Poland and Hungry.

Russia's failure to generate wealth amid an extraordinary supply of resources has its roots in the nation's history. The country has traditionally placed immense power in the hands of an authoritarian ruler. Its history is the opposite of the United States, which has a legacy of placing power and control in the hands of individuals and markets.

Russia's history of authoritarian leaders extends back to its czarist governing system. At the beginning of the 20th century the czar's role was to mediate disputes among powerful leaders who ran the economy. In 1913, this economic model enabled Russia to produce roughly 4% of the world's output. After 1913, Russia turned to communism. For the rest of the 20th century, its experiment with communism turned into an economic and a humanitarian disaster.

In 1913, Russia's wealth and efficiency, measured as output per person, is estimated to have been close to the world average and just over half the level in the US. After World War II and into the 1970s, Russia and the rest of the Soviet Union appeared to have increased its wealth. Estimates based on Russia's numbers show output per person in the 1970s reaching 70% of the US level while Russia's share of the world's output reached 5.5%. These numbers were an illusion.

Without a market economy, it's impossible to determine the real value of a nation's output. In Russia, government-owned and operated factories were not only inefficient in what they produced, they often produced things no one wanted. Moreover, defense spending accounted for more than 15% of the nation's output. All this became readily apparent after the collapse of the Soviet Union in 1991.

In the 1990s, as Russia's economy transitioned to a market system, unwanted and inefficient businesses and industries shut down. By 1998, Russia's output per person fell to less than 30% of that in the US. This is a more realistic estimate of where Russia's wealth actually had been during its experiment with communism.

Output per Person US & Russia: 1900 - 2015

2014 PPP $; log scale   (Prior to 1992 Russian data based on growth for USSR)

United States

Russia

$32,000

$16,000

$8,000

$4,000

1900 1910 1920 1930 1940 1950 1960 1970 1980 1990 2000 2010

Source: Angus Maddison, The World Economy; IMF, World Economic Outlook Database, April 2016; classicalprinciples.com

Previous chapters show how even modest moves to reduce economic freedom can undermine growth and the creation of wealth. Communism involves giving government almost complete authority to control individuals, businesses and markets. Russia's adoption of such policies completely impoverished an otherwise wealthy nation.

Following the collapse of the Soviet Union, Russia transitioned to a more market-oriented economy. Many government-owned industries were privatized. Controversy surrounded the privatization when ownership of state companies ended up in the hands of a small group of elite, wealthy businessmen. Furthermore, the government retained ownership of many "strategic" industries, including energy and defense-related companies.

As Russia's transition to a market-oriented economy continued, the nation's wealth and efficiency improved. Output per person increased from less than 30% of the level in United States in 1998, to roughly half that of the United States in 2013. In spite of this improvement, Russia's economy is a model of inefficiency. In 2015, the nation's output per person was the lowest among all the world's major developed nations.

Russia's current economic policies involve certain aspects of free-market policies along with those found in only the most authoritarian of governments. Government spending in Russia is a moderate 30% to 35% of the nation's output. Its tax system has a low, flat 13% tax on all individual income, including capital gains. Corporate rates are a moderate 20% for many businesses. These are all consistent with a free economy.

Unfortunately, Russia is not a free economy. Secure rights to private property and a just legal system are essential requirements for economic freedom. The lack of secure property rights or the rule of law, along with a culture of corruption, places Russia in the lower half of all countries in terms of economic freedom. The Fraser Institute lists Russia as 102 in the world out of 159 countries, while the Heritage Foundation lists Russia as 153rd out of 186 countries in terms of economic freedom.

In recent years, Russia appears to have reverted back to its authoritarian past. Without the rule of law or protection of private property, the country's leader rules with an iron hand. As with its czars, Russia's leader either grants or removes wealth from elite groups of wealthy people who run the economy. Even though blessed with tremendous natural resources, Russia's controlled economic system struggles to generate even half the wealth of systems that disperse power to individuals, businesses and markets.

Economic Freedom Scores: US, Russia & Poland

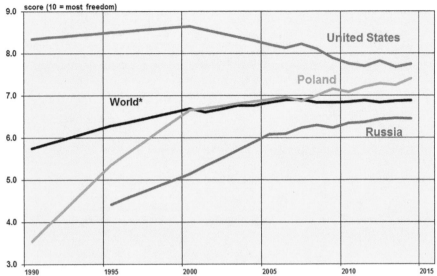

Source: Fraser Institute; Economic Freedom of the World, 2016 Annual Report; (5 year intervals until 2005);
*average of 104 countries with scores available since 1980.

Output per Person: US, Russia & Poland

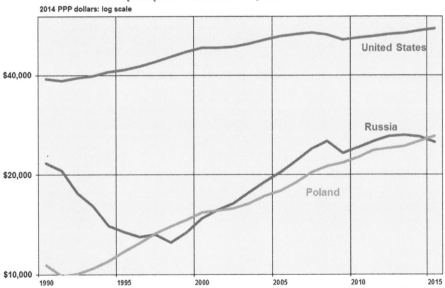

Source: International Monetary Fund, World Economic Outlook Database, April, 2016;Angus Maddison, The World
Economy; classicalprinciples.com

CHAPTER 20

Japan: The Sun Also Sets

When I was a young guy, when I first started with G.E., Jack Welch sent us all to Japan because in those days Japan was gonna crush us.
— Jeffrey Immelt

In the 1989 film, *Back to the Future II*, Marty McFly travels to the year 2015 to discover he works for a Japanese company. In 1989, there were many who believed the Japanese would soon dominate much of the world. The reason was clear. Japan was enjoying spectacular growth. After having lost World War II, the country seemingly had discovered the key to the wealth of nations.

In 1950, Japan's economy was in shambles. Output accounted for 3% of the world's total. During the next forty years, in spite of a strong rebound in the world economy, Japan's growth was even faster. By 1989, Japan's share of the world's output had increased to almost 9%. Its wealth in 1950 was only 20% of that in the United States. By 1990, Japan's wealth reached 80% of that in the United States. Moreover, Japan's increase was on a trajectory to make Japan the world's wealthiest economy.

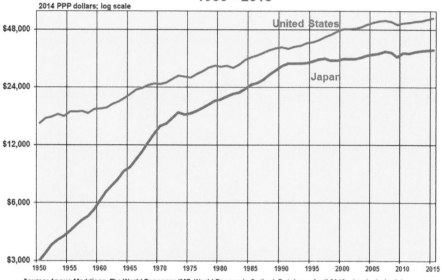

Output per Person: Japan and the United States
1950 - 2015

Source: Angus Maddison, The World Economy; IMF, World Economic Outlook Database, April 2016; classicalprinciples.com

In 1989, many observers attributed Japan's success to the government's active role in guiding its economy. The Ministry of Trade and Industry was given credit for determining economic goals, such as a doubling of steel production, and then providing the financing and other assistance to help make its goals a reality. Credit was also given to its keiretsu, a system of cooperation among businesses and banks. Others credited a system of guaranteed lifetime employment and a cooperative business-union relationship.

Japan's economic performance, both before and after 1989, indicates the nation's success had little to do with any of these popular explanations. The first and most spectacular stage of Japan's postwar growth occurred from 1950 to 1974. This stage involved rebuilding the country after the devastation of World War II. It also involved the introduction of certain aspects of free-market capitalism into what was otherwise a tightly controlled economy.

After the war, the United States had imposed extremely high, progressive tax rates on Japan in an effort to prevent large concentrations of power and wealth. In 1950, Japan began an aggressive effort to reduce these burdens by cutting the highest tax rate from 86% to 55%. In his analysis of Japan's tax policy, economist Alan Reynolds points out how, with the exception of 1960, Japan cut its tax rates every year from 1950 to 1974. As in the United States, Japan's listed tax rates overstated the rates people actually paid. The actual rates paid were relatively low due to generous exemptions and deductions.

Perhaps most important of all, Japan's tax system encouraged savings and investments. There were no taxes on capital gains from either stocks or property. Interest and dividends were also exempt from taxes. As we have seen in other countries, a zero tax on capital gains tends to be associated with rapid growth.

In addition to its tax policy, government spending was relatively low. Up to the 1970s, government spending was below 20% of national income. This was similar to that in Hong Kong and Singapore. In spite of these pro-growth policies, Japan retained numerous controls over businesses and markets. Such controls tend to limit a country's efficiency and wealth.

A surge in oil prices in 1974 adversely affected the nation's economy. In response, Japan began to move away from its low tax and limited government spending policies. Inflation pushed taxpayers into higher tax brackets increasing effective tax rates. By 1980, rapid increases in government spending raised the government's share of the nation's output to 27%.

In the 1980s, Japan's government spending increased twice as fast as spending in the rest of the economy. As we have seen in the United States and other countries, rapid growth in government spending is often associated with slower real growth. The same was the case in Japan during the 1980s.

The slower pace of growth from 1974 to 1989 was the beginning of the end for the so-called Japanese *miracle.* The end came following 1989. That was the critical year Japan introduced a series of taxes on savings and investments. For the first time, Japan imposed a capital gains tax on both stocks and property. It also imposed a tax on interest and dividends and introduced a value added tax (VAT) which applied to almost all purchases. Although the VAT was only 3%, it punished savers. It did so by reducing the buying power of all outstanding savings by the amount of the tax.

Japan's destructive tax policies were followed by an extended period of economic stagnation. The country attempted to restore growth through further massive increases in government spending. From 1989 to 1999 government spending again rose twice as fast as spending in the rest of the economy. In addition, in 1997 Japan increased its VAT to 5%, once again punishing those who had saved for the future.

The increases in government spending and taxes in Japan's economy had the same impact as similar policies in other countries. It undermined growth and limited increases in living standards.

In retrospect, Japan's economic *miracle* wasn't a miracle at all. The rapid growth in Japan following World War II and continuing into the 1980s was due to policies providing strong incentives to save and invest while limiting the growth in government spending. The sun began to set on the Japanese economy as its policies moved away from these time-tested principles for generating growth and prosperity.

In the quarter of a century prior to 1990, Japan's wealth increased by roughly 5% a year. In the quarter century since 1990, the increase was only 0.75% a year. For Japan's economy, the sun had set.

Economic Freedom: Japan and the United States

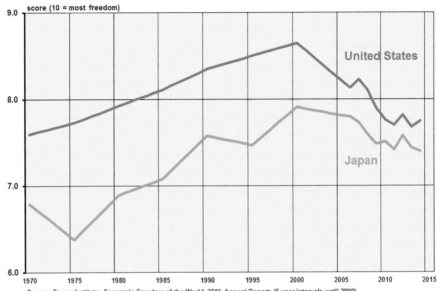

Source: Fraser Institute; Economic Freedom of the World, 2016 Annual Report; (5 year intervals until 2000)

Output per Person: Japan and the United States
1970 - 2015

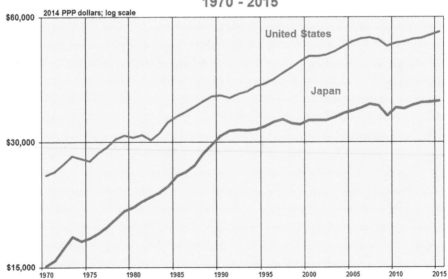

Source: Angus Maddison, The World Economy; IMF, World Economic Outlook Database, April 2016; classicalprinciples.com

CHAPTER 21

Latin America's Winners & Losers

They talk about the failure of socialism but where is the success of capitalism in Africa, Asia and Latin America? — Fidel Castro

When he wrote the *Wealth of Nations,* Adam Smith praised the performance of the British colonies. In contrast, he explained how there were a number of factors undermining growth and prosperity in Latin America's Spanish and Portuguese colonies. Smith pointed out how these colonies lacked individual freedom, granted monopoly power to special interests, had ceremonial extravagance and also had a certain penchant for violence.

Smith's emphasis on the importance of free markets and individual freedom provides one reason why Latin America developed more slowly than the United States. As recently as 1950, most of Latin America was poor. Output per person was close to the world average of $4,000, about 70% below that of the United States.

There were two exceptions to Latin America's poverty. The first was Venezuela. As a country with the world's largest oil reserves, Venezuela's output per person in 1950 amounted to $14,000, close to the United States figure of $15,000. The second wealthiest Latin country at that time was Argentina with wealth measured at $9,000 per person.

For most of the next fifty years, almost all of Latin America pursued progressive socialist policies. These consisted of government ownership or control of key industries, government sanctioned monopolies, and government control of markets and prices. In addition, there were numerous social movements designed to redistribute income and land from the rich to the poor. In the wake of such policies, Latin America experienced a history of poverty, social upheaval, dictatorships, and military coups.

As a group, Latin American countries have suffered from a lack of economic freedom. The Fraser Institute's list of economic freedom shows the average score for the eight largest countries in Latin America has consistently been below the world average. In 2014, the average economic freedom score for major Latin American countries was still 12% below the world average.

Since 1980, the two Latin American countries with the most dramatic changes in economic policies have been Venezuela and Chile. Venezuela's policies have moved away from economic freedom to almost complete government control. Using data from 2014, the Fraser Institute ranks Venezuela's economy as having the least amount of economic freedom out of the 159 countries it measures. The Heritage Foundation places Venezuela next to North Korea and Cuba and nearly at the bottom of its 186 country list.

Over the past forty years, as Venezuela moved its policies away from economic freedom, the opposite occurred in Chile. In the 1960s and early 1970s, Chile was one of the worst countries in the world in terms of economic freedom. As with many Latin American countries, Chile had a history embracing progressive socialist policies. Its critics blamed businesses and the rich for the economy's problems. Chile's government had nationalized businesses, instituted land reforms, promoted public works projects and introduced both tariffs and wage and price controls in an effort to boost its economy.

By the early 1970s, Chile's economy had collapsed into chaos. In 1973, a military coup led to a dramatic change in policies. Chile's military government called on free-market economists to help solve the nation's problems. Many of those called upon were educated at the University of Chicago under Milton Friedman, the most influential free-market classical economist since Adam Smith.

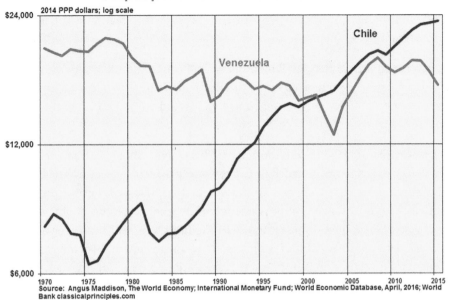

Output per Person: Chile & Venezuela

2014 PPP dollars; log scale

Source: Angus Maddison, The World Economy; International Monetary Fund; World Economic Database, April, 2016; World Bank classicalprinciples.com

Under the guidance of free-market advisors, Chile's government privatized government-owned businesses, reduced barriers to international trade and removed controls over wages and prices. Under the leadership of José Pinera, Chile privatized the nation's bankrupt social security system. A recent study shows how after 32 years, Chile's retirement funds had earned an average return of 8.7% after inflation, and are able to pay workers six times more than the government system had promised them.

Prior to 1975, Chile's economic freedom score was close to today's low score in Venezuela. Within three decades, Chile not only became the country with the highest degree of economic freedom in Latin America, it became one of the freest countries in the world. The Fraser Institute lists Chile as the 13th freest economy in the world in 2014, while the Heritage Foundation lists it as the 7th freest in 2015.

The dramatic policy shifts in both countries had an equally dramatic impact on the wealth and living standards of their people. By 2015, Venezuela's economy was in shambles, with many of its citizens unable to obtain basic necessities. The nation's output per person as reported by Venezuela's government was back to the same level as in 1955 and declining rapidly. As in the case of Russia and Argentina, government reports on economic measures in highly controlled economies tend to overstate the country's performance. In contrast to the collapse in Venezuela, Chile's economy has soared. In terms of output per person, Chile has recently overtaken Argentina to become the wealthiest economy in Latin America.

A pattern similar to that in Chile occurred in Peru in the 1990s. As with Chile, Peru's experiment with progressive socialist policies had produced an economic catastrophe. In 1990, chaos reigned as living standards collapsed and inflation soared.

The election of Alberto Fujimori in 1990 brought about a dramatic policy change. Government-owned businesses were privatized, price controls were abolished, and tariffs were cut. In the decade that followed, Peru experienced one of the most dramatic improvements in economic freedom of any country in the world. In 2009, in a testimony to Fujimori and his policies, two-thirds of Peruvians approved of his leadership. This was in spite of his conviction for human rights abuses. In 2014, Peru was the third highest Latin American country in terms of economic freedom. The following chart shows how Peru's shift to free-market classical principles was followed by a substantial improvement in economic conditions.

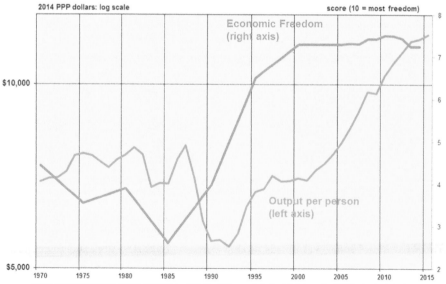

Output per Person & Economic Freedom: Peru

Source: Angus Maddison, The World Economy; IMF, World Economic Outlook Database, April 2016; classicalprinciples.com ;
: Fraser Institute; Economic Freedom of the World, 2015 Annual Report (5 year intervals until 2000)

The policy experience of other Latin American countries, particularly Argentina, is also insightful. As the charts below show, output per person appeared to have held up well in spite of a sharp decline in economic freedom since 2000. In June of 2016, the newly elected government discovered recent data had overstated growth by 18%. Revised data (not shown on the chart) will show Argentina did experience the economic harm usually associated with moves toward progressive socialist policies.

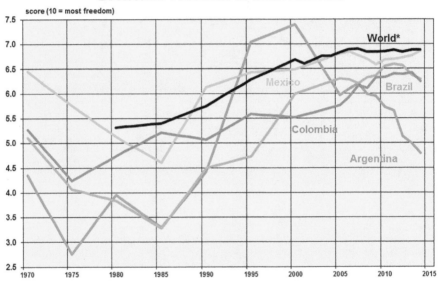

Economic Freedom in Latin America

Source: Fraser Institute, Economic Freedom of the World 2016 Annual Report; classicalprinciples.com ;
*average of 104 countries with scores since 1980

Output per Person: Latin America

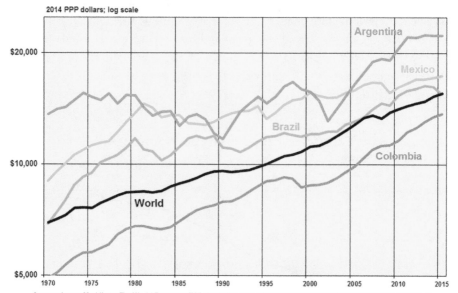

2014 PPP dollars; log scale

Source: Angus Maddison, The World Economy; IMF, World Economic Outlook Database, April 2016; classicalprinciples.com

CHAPTER 22

Africa: Lights in the Dark Continent

In Africa today, we recognize that trade and investment, and not aid, are pillars of development. — Paul Kagame, President of Rwanda

I am still a socialist. I am a left-of-center politician. I believe that in Africa, if you see the poverty around us, you can't afford to be anything else.
— John Dramani Mahama, President of Ghana

Of all the poverty in the world, the greatest is in Sub-Saharan Africa. In 2015, the average annual output per person was 75% *below* the average in Latin America and well below the Middle East.

Output per Person: Poorest Regions in the World

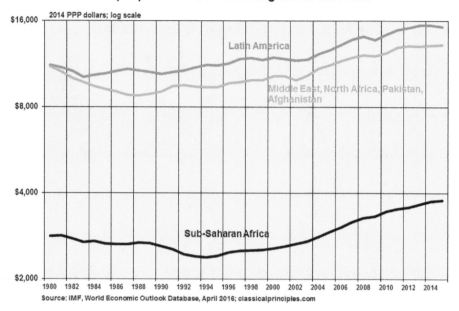

$16,000 2014 PPP dollars; log scale

Latin America

Middle East, North Africa, Pakistan, Afghanistan

$8,000

$4,000

Sub-Saharan Africa

$2,000

1980 1982 1984 1986 1988 1990 1992 1994 1996 1998 2000 2002 2004 2006 2008 2010 2012 2014

Source: IMF, World Economic Outlook Database, April 2016; classicalprinciples.com

The very magnitude of the area's poverty raises questions regarding how regional challenges, such as climate, terrain and culture, contribute to such deplorable conditions. While these factors may play a role, recent developments suggest the lack of economic freedom plays an even larger role in Africa's poverty. Historically, economic freedom has been as foreign to this part of the world as prosperity.

From 1980 to 2000, output per person in Sub-Saharan Africa fell by an average of 0.5% a year. In the poorest region in the world, poverty was getting worse. Fortunately, things began to change. From 2000 to 2015, wealth, measured as output per person, increased by 2.5% a year. As in so many other places in the world, the improvement in Sub-Saharan Africa followed increases in economic freedom.

Three of Africa's most successful countries have been Botswana, Nigeria and Ghana. Botswana, a country of only 2 million people, was the first African country to score fairly high on Fraser's measures of freedom. By the turn of the century, Botswana's score moved above the world average. This was well in advance of the improvement in the scores in some other African countries. Although Botswana's score has not improved further since 2000, it has remained relatively high. In 2015 Botswana was the only notable African country where wealth moved above the world average. Nigeria and Ghana are two other African nations that have experienced considerable improvements in economic freedom. Nigeria is particularly important since it is the largest economy in Africa, both in terms of people and output.

Nigeria experienced a major improvement in terms of economic freedom from 1996 to 2007. Within several years of this improvement, there was a dramatic increase in Nigeria's economic performance. Output per person increased an average of 5% a year from 2000 to 2012 compared to increases of only 1% a year during the 1990s. Although the country has some oil, it was not a factor in the improvement since oil contributed more to growth in the 1990s than in the more recent period.

The bad news for Nigeria is its economic freedom score remains below the world average. It has been flat to down since 2007. After a lag of a several years, there are tentative signs of a slowdown in Nigeria's economy. Time will tell the extent to which Nigeria's slower growth is related to the collapse in oil prices, or to a failure to improve its economic freedom.

There is a similar development unfolding in Ghana. Following a major improvement in Ghana's economic freedom score from 1985 to 2007, the country enjoyed substantial growth. Output per person from 1992 to 2012 rose by 4% a year. The recent decline in Ghana's freedom score is particularly significant in light of President Mahama's belief in socialism and left-leaning policies as a cure for poverty. As we have seen throughout the world, socialist policies don't alleviate poverty, they create it. As in Nigeria, Ghana's strong growth has come to an end. If the pause continues, it would be fully consistent with the country's recent move away from economic freedom.

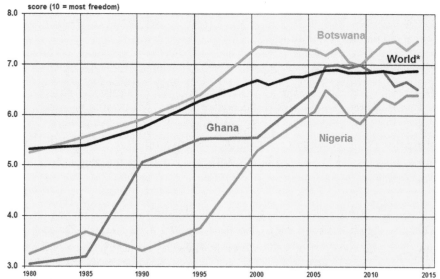

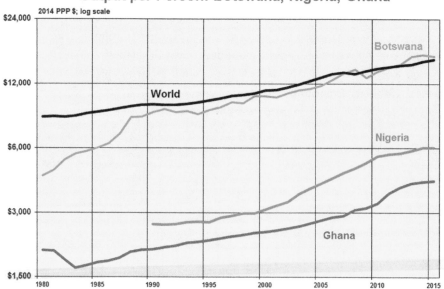

Some of the Sub-Saharan region's poorest countries are Kenya, Zambia, Uganda and Rwanda. As recently as the turn of the century, output per person in each of these four countries was below the Sub-Saharan average of $2,500. Since then, Zambia, Uganda and Rwanda have all had very sharp increases in their economic freedom scores.

In the decade ending in 2015, Zambia's growth averaged 7% a year. This was fast enough to bring its output per person slightly above the average of Sub-Saharan Africa by 2015. Over the same period, Rwanda's growth was an even stronger 7.5% a year. Its output per person grew 5% a year. In spite of these gains, Rwanda's output per person remained well below the average for Sub-Sahara Africa in 2015. This was due to starting from a very low level. Uganda also had impressive gains averaging almost 4% a year in output per person.

When exposed to economic freedom, we find Africans respond in a way that increases their living standards. As a result, when African countries move aggressively to increase economic freedom, they experience rapid growth in much the same way we observed in so many other countries. These developments strongly suggest that an almost total lack of economic freedom has contributed to the extreme poverty found in this part of the world.

The recent progress in promoting free market classical principles in the countries of Sub-Saharan Africa has important implications for the future. It indicates further aggressive increases in economic freedom in Africa can have the same beneficial impact they have had throughout the rest of the world. The path to eliminating abject poverty in Africa is apparent. All policymakers have to do is take it.

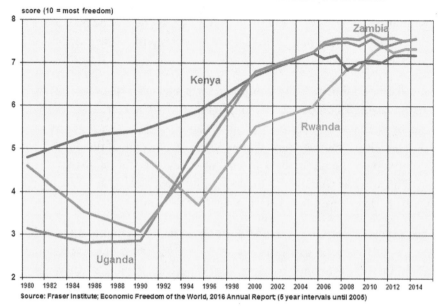

Economic Freedom: Selected African Countries

Source: Fraser Institute; Economic Freedom of the World, 2016 Annual Report; (5 year intervals until 2005)

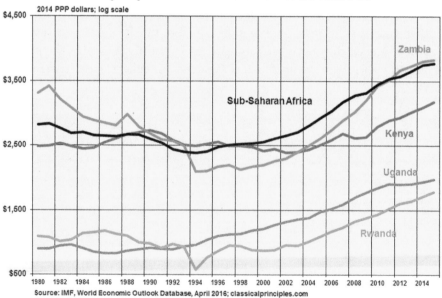

Output per Person: Select African Nations

Source: IMF, World Economic Outlook Database, April 2016; classicalprinciples.com

CHAPTER 23

Summary and Conclusions

Underlying most arguments against the free market is a lack of belief in freedom itself.
— Milton Friedman

The objective of this book has been to present evidence on why some nations are rich and others poor. Following the lead of history's most famous economists, our approach examined the policies of nations from the perspective of economic freedom. Such a policy-oriented approach produces actionable advice to policy-makers and advocates.

We observed the extent to which policies either promote or impede economic freedom in forty key countries throughout the world. We then observed the extent to which these policies were associated with each country's subsequent economic performance.

In the process, we have taken a journey back in time, through mountains of data, and across a diversified mix of countries, large and small, rich and poor. This extensive analysis leads to the following general conclusions:

In spite of the broad diversity among people and nations, there is one commonality that stands out— people throughout the world are remarkably similar in how they respond to economic policies. Regardless of their culture, people respond to policies promoting economic freedom in the most creative and productive ways imaginable. This response consistently enhances the wealth of individuals and, in turn, the wealth of their nations.

In contrast, policies restricting economic freedom repress people's creative, productive behavior. As a result, such policies consistently undermine the creation of wealth, both for individuals and their countries.

The analysis also reveals how the effects of economic policies have a compounding effect over time. The higher a country's degree of economic freedom, and the longer it is sustained, the greater the increase in a country's wealth. In a similar manner, the longer and further policies move away from such freedom, the more countries experience widespread poverty.

Time and again we found a direct association between significant changes in economic policies and significant changes in the wealth of nations. The data show dramatic policy changes toward free-market classical policies tend to be followed by equally dramatic increases in wealth. In a similar manner, significant policy shifts away from such freedom tend to be followed by significant adverse impacts on wealth.

These results are similar regardless of a country's size or location, or whether the country is rich or poor. We also noted how many of the world's developed countries were recently moving policies away from economic freedom, while many poorer countries were moving toward such freedom. Based on these trends, we would expect developed nations to continue to experience sluggish growth, while certain poorer nations will experience some relief from poverty.

As for developments in specific countries, we saw how the United States rapidly became the world's wealthiest and largest economy by maximizing economic freedom. In spite of its unprecedented success, for the past century economic policies in the United States have alternated between cycles of more and less freedom.

Analyzing policy cycles in the United States since 1900 shows almost all growth in after-tax wages occurred during periods when economic policies were moving in the direction of free-market classical policies. These policies consist of low or declining tax rates, particularly for investors and those with higher incomes, slow growth in government spending relative to total spending, and less government control over individuals, businesses and markets.

In contrast, we found no improvement in after-tax wages when policies move in the opposite direction. Such periods involved policies where government expanded its control over the behavior of individuals, businesses and markets, increased its spending relative to the private sector, and raised taxes, particularly on investors and those with higher incomes.

Shifting from the United States to other countries we found the response to policies affecting economic freedom is much the same as in the United States. Countries whose policies persistently embraced greater economic freedom become progressively wealthier. Specifically, the consistent application of free-market classical policies in Singapore and Hong Kong was associated with transforming these nations from poverty to wealth.

We observed how China's deliberate shift toward free-market classical principles enabled it to become an economic powerhouse within the span of a few decades. By transforming one of the world's largest and poorest economies, China shows how breaking the cycle of extreme poverty is possible.

In contrast, we show how the more a nation's policies move away from economic freedom, the more it undermines wealth and promotes poverty. In the extreme, we saw how policies that maximize government control over the lives of individuals, as in Russia and Venezuela, impoverished once wealthy nations.

Analyzing data from forty countries over an extensive period of history has many advantages. It enabled us to observe how recent policy shifts toward economic freedom are similar to and as effective in improving wealth as shifts in other countries and in earlier times. The recent experience in certain African countries shows how abrupt shifts toward freedom today are similar to responses we observed in Chile and Peru, thirty and forty years ago. In spite of the passage of time, people's response to freedom has not changed.

Adam Smith and Milton Friedman emphasized the importance of economic freedom to creating prosperity. Our analysis confirms their insights. The preponderance of evidence leaves little doubt about the role of economic freedom in promoting the wealth of nations, while the lack of such freedom promotes poverty.

Freedom places individuals in charge of and responsible for their own accomplishments. Given freedom, individuals respond by unleashing their creative potential and maximizing their God-given talents. It is in unleashing this creative potential that we find the true force behind enhancing the wealth of nations.

Data Appendices

Some General Comments

In my research for this book I compiled a great deal of data, much of it going back to 1900 and some going back to 1820. All economic data are only rough estimates of economic concepts. All data have shortcomings. The further back in history we go, the less reliable the data.

For the US we have reasonably consistent data going back to 1929. Prior to 1929 the data are far less reliable. In my efforts to provide a consistent series going back further than 1929, I had to make a number of assumptions and adjustments. These may contain serious shortcomings.

All researchers have their biases. My bias is a belief in the importance of economic freedom. After years of observing the financial pain and suffering from policies that erode such freedom, it's difficult for me to ignore what appears obvious. However, for research and analysis to be legitimate and useful, it must overcome any influence from the researcher's bias. I spent several years organizing the data before attempting to draw any conclusions.

Once the data were organized, I was surprised to find the extent of damage from government policies was as great as it was. I was also surprised to find how similar the impact has been throughout history and throughout the world.

At various points in my research, I attempted to disprove my bias in favor of free-market classical principles. On several occasions I thought I had succeeded. One was when I discovered how poor Chile was today compared to the United States. Since I knew Chile had adopted free-market policies back in the 1980s, I assumed I had found an example of how such policies had failed. However, in charting the country's policy shift and its economic response, it became obvious Chile's extraordinary growth had come from an extremely low level of wealth. There were normal lags between changing policies and observing results. Chile needed time to rebuild the nation's infrastructure, which had been severely damaged from prior progressive, socialist policies. While Chile's wealth may be low relative to many other countries in the world, its progress since the 1980s has been extremely impressive.

A similar development occurred with respect to Argentina. Recent measures of economic freedom suggested the economy should be doing much worse than the data indicated. I thought I had found another case where government controls were not nearly as damaging as they had been in other countries. Recently, Argentina's data was extensively revised to show there was more damage than originally reported.

A third case, which may yet prove to be the exception to the rule, is with the Middle East Kingdom of Jordan. Based on its data from 2014, the Fraser Institute ranks Jordan as the 14th freest country in the world. The nation's output per person for 2015 was $12,000, or about $3,500 below the world average. This time, I thought I had the exception to the rule of economic freedom producing prosperity.

I compared the Fraser Institute's data for Jordan's economic freedom to that of Israel and matched it to each country's output per person. Israel's output per person has been consistently higher than that in Jordan in spite of Jordan's economic freedom scores being at or above Israel's scores. Although the results are inconsistent with most other countries, there are two caveats. First, the Heritage Foundation measures of economic freedom show Israel as the 35th freest country and Jordan as the 46th freest.

Hence, there is a discrepancy with respect to which country has the higher degree of economic freedom. In addition, when I checked for consistency of percent changes between the IMF and Angus data for output per person during overlap periods, the data were inconsistent.

While the discrepancy between these countries may be attributed to problems with data, it would not be surprising to find factors other than economic freedom influencing a nation's performance. An influx of refugees into Jordan due to the war in Syria provides an example of how factors other than economic freedom can prevent a nation from achieving prosperity. While there are certain things policymakers cannot control, the degree of economic freedom can be controlled. Based on the experience a vast majority of all countries, it would appear that greater economic freedom would be the appropriate policy for minimizing poverty associated with uncontrollable events.

Economic Freedom: Israel & Jordan

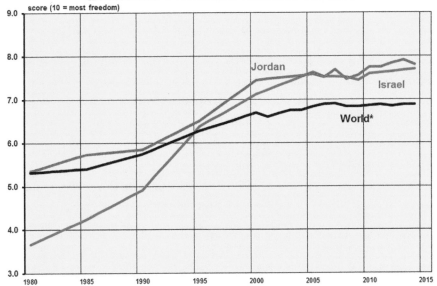

Source: Fraser Institute; Economic Freedom of the World, 2016 Annual Report; (5 year intervals until 2000)' average of 104 countries with scores since 1980

Output per Person: Israel & Jordan

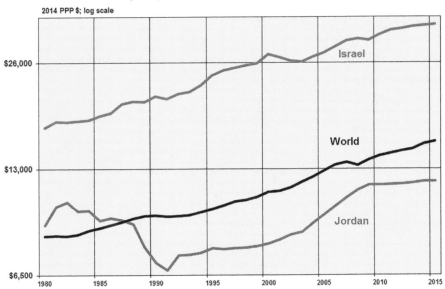

Source: Angus Maddison, The World Economy; IMF, World Economic Outlook Database, April 2016; classicalprinciples.com

APPENDIX A NOTES ON WAGES & SALARIES

One of the most challenging things to measure is the wage or salary of a typical or median worker. Any such number will never be more than a very rough estimate. I prefer the term typical to the more precise term median as a way of communicating to those not readily familiar with the latter term.

All attempts to find the wages and salaries of a typical (i.e. median) worker suffer from key problems. One of the most important is the data involve surveys where individuals are asked to provide information about their wages. The results assume individuals know their wages, and people are telling the truth.

Taking these assumptions as given, the next challenge is to determine the characteristics of the typical worker. The US Bureau of Labor Statistics (BLS) has detailed information on median wages and salaries for individuals based on a number of characteristics, including education. All categories include individuals 25 years old and older. This eliminates the bias due to including younger, lower paid, less experienced individuals. Such individuals are not likely to be characteristic of what most people think of as typical. The following chart shows BLS data for typical or median workers as well as average wages for production and nonsupervisory employees.

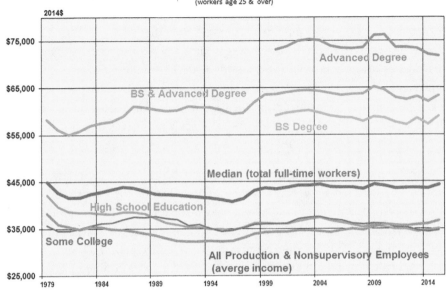

Median Annual Income by Educational Achievement
(workers age 25 & over)

Source: US BLS, CPS; income defined as annual wages and salaries; classicalprinciples.com

The median wage for *all* full-time workers is the most comprehensive of all these groups. It shows the annual wages of a typical worker before taxes. Since 1979, this level has been at or slightly below $45,000 a year after adjusting for inflation. Interestingly, the only category to experience any increase since 1979 are those with a college degree. However, this category has experienced a decline since the late 1990s. Since 2004, the only category to experience an increase is the average wage for production and nonsupervisory employees. This is also the group that experienced the largest decline in the 1980s and early 1990s.

It is informative to compare the results of the median surveys to those based on income tax returns, which involve *hard* data. The US Bureau of Economic Analysis (BEA) defines employee wages and salaries in terms of three components—total compensation, pre-tax wages and salaries, and wages and salaries after personal taxes.

Personal taxes consist of individual income taxes and Social Security contributions paid from both individuals and their employer. While few individuals consider the employer contribution as part of their contribution, businesses are indifferent to whether they have to pay a certain amount as a wage or as a tax. Every business person and economist understands, or should understand, how the employer payment for mandated costs, such as Social Security, is actually part of employee compensation.

To determine the average employee's income from these data, we take total employee compensation, total worker wages and salaries, and total worker wages and salaries less all personal taxes and divide each by the number of full-time equivalent employees. The data covering the years 1929 to the present are all readily available for download from the BEA website. The following chart shows the relationship among these categories, alongside the survey data for the median wages and salaries for all full-time workers 25 years and older.

The following chart reveals several important things about both the average worker and the median worker's compensation. The first is how all three measures of average compensation have increased since 1979, with fairly substantial increases in total compensation and pretax wages. It also shows large differences between average and median measures over the entire period. However, there are similarities during subperiods. All measures of income declined sharply from 1979 to 1981. All measures increased from 1981-1986 and from 1996- 2004. All measures had their worst performances from 1986 to1996 and from 2004 to 2015.

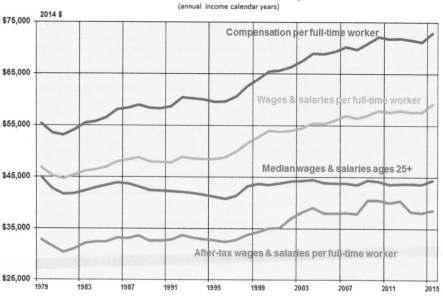

Measures of Full-time Worker Earnings 1979 - 2015
(annual income calendar years)

Source: US Bureau of Economic Analysis; US Bureau of Labor Statistics; classicalprinciples.com

This is similar to the trends noted in the chart of median income by education. During periods when the economy performs well, workers with all levels of educational attainment do better than when the economy is performing poorly. This pattern leads to two important conclusions.

One conclusion is there is no precise way to estimate median income. Income tax rates, tax-deferred income and Social Security tax changes all make it difficult to use recent median income data as a guide to median income prior to 1979. However, the tendency for all measures to move in the same direction during subperiods strongly suggests the use of average wages can provide a reliable guide to the direction of a median worker's income.

For my primary analysis of economic conditions in the United States, I use the average wage after all personal taxes. This is the wage most workers can identify with, since it represents the income they directly control. It is particularly relevant for low income or temporary workers. These workers tend to receive progressively less from benefits, such as IRAs or other retirement benefits, than higher paid workers.

Appendix B GDP per person as a Guide to Wages & Salaries

Gross Domestic Product (GDP) per person is often used as an estimate of a country's productivity. A more accurate measure would be output per worker or per hour worked. When analyzing activity within the US, where historical data for both wages and full-time equivalent employees are available, we use these numbers instead of either GDP or population. However, when comparing the US to other nations, we use the more common GDP per person measures *adjusted for purchasing power parity.*

GDP per person should tend to capture changes in a nation's productivity since population tends to change slowly over time. And changes in productivity, in turn, should capture changes in wages. There are many reasons why such general tendencies do not hold with the use of actual data. Measures of output (GDP) are only rough, imprecise estimates of a theoretical concept. Even if measured accurately, GDP is significantly higher than wages since it includes profits, rents, interest receipts and depreciation expenses. As an offset, population data are significantly higher than the number of employees. Since these differences tend to offset each other, it is possible for GDP per capita to be a rough guide to both productivity and workers' wages.

While international comparisons of GDP per capita can provide a rough guide for differences in workers' salaries in different countries, it's important to recognize potential differences. The following chart shows the relationship between GDP per capita and various measures of employee earnings since 1929. It shows even though GDP per capita has recently been a reasonably close measure of average pre-tax wages and salaries, this hasn't always been the case. The relationship becomes progressively different as we move further into the past.

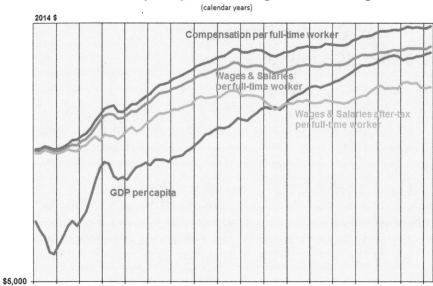

GDP per Capita and Average Worker Earnings
(calendar years)

2014 $

Compensation per full-time worker

Wages & Salaries per full-time worker

Wages & Salaries after-tax per full-time worker

GDP per capita

$5,000

1929 1934 1939 1944 1949 1954 1959 1964 1969 1974 1979 1984 1989 1994 1999 2004 2009 2014

Source: US Census; Bureau of Economic Analysis; classicalprinciples.com

APPENDIX C IDENTIFYING CLASSICAL AND PROGRESSIVE PERIODS

Choosing the starting and ending dates for periods of classical or progressive policies is a challenge. The primary criterion for dating these periods is the direction of policies. The commentary contained in various chapters provides most of the rationale for choosing specific years. In addition to the direction of economic policies, whenever possible, an attempt was made to shift the beginning and end of the policy periods to make them consistent with similar stages of the business cycle. This was accomplished in many cases by starting and ending the periods with similar unemployment rates so as to avoid a cyclical bias. Beginning a period at a time of low unemployment and ending it at a time of high unemployment provides a negative cyclical bias that may be unrelated to the longer-term secular trend.

It wasn't always easy to avoid the problem of cyclical bias since the unemployment rates tended to increase at the end of progressive periods. This was the case in 1920, 1940 and 1981.

For example, during the progressive period of 1913-20, it is tempting to list the year ending in June, 1921 as the end of the period. Most tax cuts did not take effect until after the fiscal year 1921 had ended. However, the unemployment rate in 1921 was 8.5%. Choosing 1921 would make the first progressive period look even worse than it was and make the recovery in the 1920s look much stronger. As it was, the unemployment rate in fiscal 1920 was more than a percentage point below the rate in 1913. This produced a positive cyclical bias in favor of the first progressive movement as well as a slight negative bias to the growth rates for the 1920s.

World War II created another such conflict. I decided to end the progressive period in 1940 due to the unique circumstances associated with the war. Although the immediate aftermath of World War II produced a major policy change consistent with classical principles, the transition from wartime to peacetime production also appeared so unique as to not be characteristic of a normal policy change. The 1948-53 designation of *ambivalent* was due to the combination of another war and a mix of both progressive and classical policies.

The period 1965-81 is another example where progressive policies ended with both a clear change in the direction of economic policies as well as a relatively high unemployment rate. To reaffirm the longer-term trends during this period, as well as 1929-40, the following tables offer alternative dates within or outside these periods where unemployment rates were similar. These dates confirm a similar deterioration during these progressive periods even after we adjust for any cyclical bias from ending the periods in either 1940 or 1981.

The same situation occurs in the period from 1981-88, where the unemployment rate in 1988 is well below the rate in 1981. I show the numbers for an alternative period from 1981-85 where the unemployment rates are the same, therefore removing any cyclical bias. The fundamental shift to recovery in the Reagan years is still apparent after this adjustment.

The dates for labeling the 1981-88, 1988-95 and 2004-15 periods were chosen based on both the timing of policy changes as well as a desire to have similar unemployment rates at both the beginning and end of the periods.

Dashboard of Economic Performance: 1900 - 1946
US Economic Performance: Classical vs Progressive Policies
(fiscal years: annual percent changes)

	1900-13	1913-20	1920-29	1929-40	1929-43	1929-46
Economic Policies:						
Federal spending growth less GDP grov	-3.7	24.6	-9.1	10.8	21.5	13.5
Federal Nondefense growth vs. GDP	-4.3	15.8	-1.2	11.4	7.6	5.2
Tax changes ⬆ or ⬇	⬇	⬆	⬇	⬆	⬆	⬆
Regulatory Policies	⬇	⬆	⬇	⬆	⬆	⬆
GDP (current $)	6.2	12.1	1.6	-0.2	4.4	4.9
Federal Spending (current $)	2.5	36.6	-7.6	10.6	25.9	18.4
Nondefense (current $)	1.9	27.9	0.3	11.2	12.0	10.1
Defense (current $)	3.3	45.3	-17.7	8.2	38.5	27.4
Economic Performance:						
(constant $)						
Consumer spending per person	2.9	0.8	1.0	0.5	1.0	2.0
Consumer spending per worker	2.6	0.9	1.5	0.7	-0.8	0.7
Compensation per worker	2.5	0.9	1.5	1.6	2.6	2.8
Wages & salaries per worker	2.4	0.9	1.5	1.3	2.2	2.4
After-tax wages per worker	2.4	0.2	1.8	0.9	0.7	1.3
GDP per person	2.5	1.6	0.3	0.8	3.7	3.3
GDP per worker	2.2	1.7	0.8	1.0	1.9	2.1
Unemployment rate percent:						
at beginning and end of period	5.0-4.5	4.5-3.3	3.3-3.7	3.7-15.9	3.7-3.3	3.7-2.9
average during period	4.7	4.8	4.6	16.2	14.5	12.4

Dashboard of Economic Performance: 1940 - 1773
US Economic Performance: Classical vs Progressive Policies
(fiscal years: dollars are 2014$ unless noted; annual percent changes)

	1940-45	1945-48	1948-53	1953-65	1965-81	1965-73
Economic Policies:						
Federal spending growth less GDP growth	39.6	-29.5	4.5	-0.9	1.8	2.7
Federal Nondefense growth vs. GDP	-13.6	41.8	-17.3	6.2	3.8	5.9
Tax changes ↑ or ↓	→	→	→	↓	↑	↑
Regulatory Policies	→	→	→	↓	↑	↑
GDP (current $)	18.2	5.0	7.8	5.3	9.7	8.4
Federal Spending (current $)	57.8	-24.5	12.4	4.4	11.5	11.1
Nondefense (current $)	4.5	46.9	-9.4	11.5	13.6	14.3
Defense (current $)	118.7	-52.1	42.1	-0.4	7.4	5.3
Economic Performance:						
(constant $)						
Consumer spending per person	4.1	2.5	1.5	2.3	1.8	3.1
Consumer spending per worker	-2.5	8.6	0.7	2.9	0.6	1.8
Compensation per worker	5.8	-1.6	3.2	2.8	0.7	2.2
Wages & salaries per worker	5.5	-1.5	2.9	2.6	0.3	4.3
After-tax wages per worker	2.1	-0.3	2.3	2.4	-0.7	0.8
GDP per person	11.6	-5.4	3.1	1.8	2.4	3.0
GDP per worker	4.5	0.2	2.4	2.3	1.2	1.7
Unemployment rate percent:						
at beginning and end of period	15.9-1.6	1.6-3.8	3.8-2.8	2.8-4.9	4.4-7.4	4.9-5.2
average during period	7.0	3.0	4.1	5.1	5.6	4.5

Dashboard of Economic Performance: 1975 - 2015
US Economic Performance: Classical vs Progressive Policies
(fiscal years: dollars are 2014$ unless noted; annual percent changes)

	1975-81	1981-85	1981-88	1988-95	1995-04	2004-15
Economic Policies:						
Federal spending growth less GDP growth	0.3	0.6	0.6	0.2	-1.1	1.2
Federal Nondefense growth vs. GDP	0.7	-0.6	-0.6	2.1	-1.4	1.6
Tax changes ↑ or ↓	↑	↓	↓	↑	↓	↑
Regulatory Policies	↑	↓	↓	↑	↓	↑
GDP (current $)	11.8	8.0	7.6	5.7	5.3	3.6
Federal Spending (current $)	12.0	8.6	8.2	5.9	4.2	4.7
Nondefense (current $)	12.5	7.4	7.1	7.8	3.9	5.2
Defense (current $)	10.5	12.5	11.7	-0.9	5.9	2.5
Economic Performance:						
(constant $)						
Consumer spending per person	1.1	3.0	3.1	1.0	2.2	0.7
Consumer spending per worker	-0.2	2.8	2.6	0.8	1.9	0.9
Compensation per worker	-0.5	1.5	1.6	0.1	1.5	0.5
Wages & salaries per worker	-0.9	1.1	1.2	0.0	1.4	0.6
After-tax wages per worker	-2.3	2.7	1.6	-0.5	1.9	-0.1
GDP per person	2.5	2.4	2.5	1.5	2.3	0.7
GDP per worker	1.2	2.1	2.0	1.4	2.0	0.9
Unemployment rate percent:						
at beginning and end of period	7.3-7.4	7.4-7.3	7.4-5.6	5.6-5.6	5.6-5.6	5.6-5.5
average during period	7.0	8.3	7.6	6.2	5.1	6.7

Appendix D International Comparisons

There are many issues associated with comparing income or wealth among nations. One obvious problem is how each nation measures its activity in terms of its own currency. The conventional approach is to adjust data for the purchasing power of an international dollar, which is actually the US dollar.

While currency exchange rates can be used for the adjustment, they don't measure what we would like to measure. Exchange rates show how much of one country's currency we can get for the other country's currency at some point in time. This doesn't tell us how the living standards or wealth in one country might compare to others. For making such comparisons we would like to know how many US dollars it would take to purchase a similar basket of goods and services in each country.

For example, if someone in the US can buy a certain basket of goods for $10,000 and someone in another country can buy the same basket for 5,000 units of their currency, it means that their currency has twice the purchasing power of a US dollar. Since the purchasing power of the other country's currency is twice that of the US dollar, it takes only half of that country's currency to buy a similar basket of goods. A ratio of 2 of the country's currency units to 1 US dollar will adjust output from that country into US dollars.

Purchasing power parity (PPP) is the term used to adjust the value of a nation's output in an attempt to provide a more accurate comparison of people's buying power across countries. It is the method used for most international comparisons. In addition to adjusting for differences in the value of a country's currency, there are efforts made to adjust for similar baskets of goods. As a result of differences in culture, housing and other factors, creating similar baskets of goods can be challenging. Efforts to overcome these challenges are undertaken by a number of international organizations to provide the analysis for creating the PPP adjustments. The specific sources for these adjustments are the Organization for Economic Cooperation and Development, the World Bank and the Penn World Tables.

The International Monetary Fund provides PPP estimates of gross domestic output (GDP) for most countries in the world. The only exceptions are countries such as North Korea and Cuba, where data are either not available or not reliable. GDP estimates are presented in current PPP international (US) dollars. The

US is the reference country and all PPP adjustments for other countries are presented as estimates relative to the US.

The IMF presents both GDP and GDP per capita time series for each country in current PPP dollars. For my purposes it's important to show real or constant dollar changes in output per person. To convert current dollars to constant dollars I use the GDP deflator for the US. This is appropriate since the US is the numeraire country.

IMF data adjusted for PPP are available beginning with 1980. For years prior to 1980 I use the changes in constant dollar PPP estimates of GDP per capita presented by Angus Maddison, in *The World Economy.* For the years 1980 to 2001, where the Maddison data overlap with the IMF data, I compared the percent changes in both series. In almost all cases the estimates of percent changes are similar. Significant differences in the overlapping years tend to occur with respect to countries such as China and Russia. These economies were controlled economies for much of the overlap period. There is often a large difference among researchers when estimating the output of economies largely controlled by governments instead of markets.

APPENDIX E MEASURES OF ECONOMIC FREEDOM

The Fraser Institute and the Heritage Foundation measures of economic free-dom are the best summary measures available for quantifying the presence of free-market classical principles among countries. There is a good deal of agree-ment with these measures when applied to the more advanced, developed na-tions. There is less agreement with respect to lesser developed nations.

Even with respect to developed nations, there are potential issues with some measures. For example, since the Fraser Institute's criteria base data on official reports, they have to accept reported tax rates when measuring taxes. On several occasions, these rates can differ significantly from the tax rates people actually pay. Tax rates actually paid are often different due to adjustments for inflation and deductions. However, since the rates actually paid are not part of official government reports, they cannot be used. Hence, we find the Fraser measures of economic freedom for the United States increasing during the late 1970s. As I note in the text, this period was clearly one of the nation's worst experiences with moves away from economic freedom due to *high effective tax rates, controls on oil and gasoline prices and a highly unstable monetary policy.*

In spite of occasions where my analysis may have reached a different conclusion than those in the Fraser data, I used these data without making any adjustments.

US Spending & Compensation: 1900 - 1915

(2014$; fiscal years)

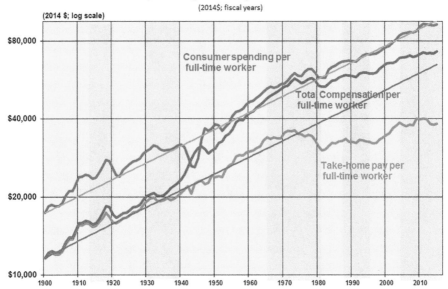

Source: US Census; BEA; BLS; Historical Statistics of the US; classicalprinciples.com ; shaded areas represent periods of progressive policies

Federal Spending per Worker: 1900-2015

(full-time workers; fiscal years)

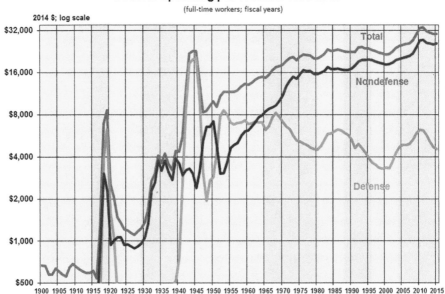

Source: US Office of Management & Budget ; classicalprinciples.com ; shaded areas represents progressive policy periods.

Bibliography

Brown, Sherrod. *Myths of Free Trade*. New York: The New Press, 2004-2006.

Brunner, Robert F. "The Dynamics of a Financial Crisis: The Panic of 1907 and the Subprime Crisis." Working Paper. 2009.

Census, US Bureau. *Historical Statistics of the United States*: 1789-1945. Washington, DC: US Government, 1949.

Census, US Bureau of the. *Historical Statistics of the United States: Colonial times to 1970 Parts 1 & 2*. Washington, DC: US Government Printing Office, 1975.

"China Construction: Importance of Infrastructure Construction in China." *IHS Global Insight* 15 January 2009.

Commission, European. "Trade Countries and Regions: Norway." 2016.

Committee, United States Senate Budget. "CRS Report: Welfare Spending The Largest Item In The Federal Budget." (n.d.).

Cowen, Tyler & Crampton, Eric. *Market Failure or Success The New Debate*. Chletenham UK: The Independent Institute, 2002

Curry, Timothy and Shibut, Lynn. "The Cost of the Savings and Loan Crisis." *FDIC Banking Review (Fall 2000): Vol. 13, No. 2*.

Devereux, Charlie. "Argentina Overhauls GDP Data, Confirming Economy in Recession." *Bloomberg* 29 June 2016.

Editorial. "Yes, Chile's Private Pension Model Works, Big Time ." *Investor's Business Daily* 26 September 2013.

Edwards, Chris. "We Can Cut Government: Canada Did." MAY/JUNE 2012.

Epstein, Richard A. *Takings*. Cambridge, Massachusetts: Harvard University Press, 1985.

Fisher, Irving. *The Rate of Interest.* New York: Macmillan, 1907.

Fisher, Irving. *The Nature of Capital and Income.* London: The Macmillan Company, 1930.

Foundation, The Heritage. *Index of Economic Freedom.* Washington, DC: The Heritage Foundation, 2016.

Friedman, Milton & Rose. *Free to Choose.* New York, London: Harcourt Brace Jovanovich, 1980.

Friedman, Milton and Schwartz, Anna Jacobson. *A Monetary History of the United States 1867-1960.* Princeton: Princeton University Press, 1963.

Genetski, Robert. *Taking the Voodoo out of Economics.* Lake Bluff, IL: Regnery Books, 1986.
Genetski, Robert. *Classical Economic Principles & the Wealth of Nations.* Cambell, CA: FastPencil, 2011. Genetski, Robert J. *A Nation of Millionaires.* Lanham, Maryland: Madison Books, 1997.
Gessen, Masha. "The Myth of the Russian Oligarchs." *The New York Times* 10 December 2014. Goldberg, Jonah. *Liberal Fascism.* New York: Broadway Books, 2007, 2009.
Hayed, Friedrich A. *The Road to Serfdom.* Chicago: The University of Chicago Press, 1944.

Holcombe, Randall G. "The Growth of the Federal Government in the 1920s." *The Cato Journal* (n.d.): Vol. 16, No. 2.

Homma, Masaaki. "Tax Reform in Japan." Takatoshi Ito and Anne O. Krueger, editors. *The Political Economy of Tax Reform, NBER-EASE Volume.* Chicago: University of Chicago Press, 1992. 69-95.

Hopkins, Thomas D. *Regulatory Costs in Profile.* St. Louis: Center for the Study of American Business, 1996.

Horwitz, Steven. "Hoover's Economic Policies." *The Concise Encyclopedia of Economics* (2008). Houghton, Jonathan and Khandker, Shahidur R. *Handbook on Poverty and Inequality.* Washington, DC:

The World Bank, 2009.

IRS. *Statistics of Income.* Washington, DC: US Government, various years.

Iversen, Carl. *International Capital Movements.* New York: Augustus M. Kelley, 1935.

James Gwartney, Robert Lawson & Joshua Hall. *Economic Freedom of the World.* Vancouver: Fraser Institute, 2013 - 2016.

Johnston, David Cay. *Free Lunch.* London: Penguin Books, 2007.

Kindleberger, Charles P. *Maniacs, Panics, and Crashes.* New York: Wiley & Sons, 1978.

Konczal, Mike. "No, we don't spend $1 trillion on welfare each year." *The Washington Post* 12 January 2014.

Krugman, Paul. *The Conscience of a Liberal.* New York: W.W. Norton & Co., 2007.

Lawler, Joseph. "About That $1 Trillion in Welfare Spending." *Real Clear Policy* 1 April 2013.

Locke, John. *Two Treatises on Government.* London: C. Baldwin, Printer (books.google.com, 1690, New Edition 1824.

Machan, Tibor. *Private Rights & Public Illusions.* New Brunswick, New Jersey: Transaction Publishers; The Independence Institute, 1995.

Maddison, Angus. *The World Economy.* Paris: OECD, 2006.
Mitchell, Daniel J. "How to Measure the Revenue Impact of Tax Changes." *The Heritage Foundation Backgrounder* 9 August 1996.

Neustadt, Richard E. and May, Ernest R. *Thinking in Time.* New York: The Free Press, 1986.

Pestritto, Ronald J. "Woodrow Wilson: Godfather of Liberalism." *Makers of American Political Thought Series #1 on Political Thought* 31 July 2012.

Piketty, Thomas. *Capital in the Twenty-First Century.* Cambridge: The Belknap Press of Harvard University Press, 2014.

Powell, Benjamin, ed. *Making Poor Nations Rich.* Stanford: Stanford University Press, 2008.
Powell, Jim. "John Locke Natural Rights to Life, Liberty and Property." *Freeman: Ideas on Liberty* August 1996.
Press, The Associated. "Peru court sentences Fujimori to 25 years in prison for

'dirty war'." *The Canadian Press* 7 April 2009.

Rajagopalan, Shruti. "India's Socialist Constitution." *The Wall Street Journal* 22 January 2008.

Reynolds, Alan. "Toward Meaningful Tax Reform in Japan." *Cato Institute* 6 April 1998.

Scientists, Federation of American. *Russian Military Budget*. NA: Federation of American Scientists, NA.

Shibut, Timothy Curry and Lynn. "The Cost of the Savings & Loan Crisis." *FDIC Banking Review* (2000). —. "The Cost of the Savings and Loan Crisis." *FDIC Banking Review* (Fall, 2000).

Shlaes, Amity. *The Forgotten Man*. New York: HarberCollins, 2007.

Shlaes, Amity. *Coolidge*. New York: HarperCollins, 2013.

Singapore, Ministry of Health. "Costs and Financing." 2013.

Smith, Adam. *An Inquiry into the Nature and Causes of the Wealth of Nations*. New York: The Modern Library Edition, 1937.

Sowell, Thomas. *On Classical Economics*. New Haven & London: Yale University Press, 2006.

Sowell, Thomas. *Basic Economics*. New York: Basic Books, 2007.

Sprinkel, Beryl W. and Genetski, Robert J. *Winning With Money*. Homewood, IL: Dow Jones-Irwin, 1977.

Sprinkel, Beryl W. and Genetski, Robert J. *Winning With Money*. Homewook, IL: Dow Jones-Irwin, 1977.

Sumner, Scott. *The Midas Paradox*. Oakland: Independent Institute, 2015.

Suzuki, Takaaki. *Japan's Budget Politics*. Boulder, Colorado: Lynne Rienner, 2000.

Tanner, Michael D. "The American Welfare State: How We Spend Nearly $1 Trillion a Year Fighting Poverty—And Fail." *Cato Institute Policy Analysis* No. 694 (April 11, 2012).

Vedder, Richard K. and Gallaway, Lowell E. Out of Work: *Unemployment and Government in Twentieth Century America (updated edition)*. New York and London: The Independent Institute, 1993, 1997.

Wanniski, Jude. *The Way the World Works.* New York: Simon & Schuster, 1978, 1983.

Weiss, Andrew S. "Russia's Oligarchy, Alive and Well." *The New York Times* 30 December 2013: opinion pages.

Williams, Walter E. "Self-Inflicted Poverty." *Townhall* 16 February 2011.